BLIZZARD'S
GARDEN
WOODWORK

BLIZZARD'S
GARDEN
WOODWORK

Richard Blizzard

WARD LOCK

A WARD LOCK BOOK

First published in the UK 1996
by Ward Lock
Wellington House
125 Strand
LONDON
WC2R 0BB

A Cassell Imprint

Text copyright © Richard Blizzard 1996
Three-dimensional illustrations © Robin Griggs
Black and white line drawings © Peter Ramsden and Richard Blizzard
Designed by Anne Fisher

Distributed in the United States
by Sterling Publishing Co., Inc.
387 Park Avenue South, New York, NY 10016-8810

A British Library Cataloguing in Publication Data block for this book
may be obtained from the British Library

ISBN 0–7063–7511–4
Typeset by Business Color Print, Welshpool, Powys, Wales
Printed and bound in Slovenia

DISCLAIMER
While every care has been taken to ensure that the information given
here is accurate, readers should check their dimensions as work
proceeds to see that they comply with the cutting lists. Neither
the author nor the publisher can be responsible for accidents, injury
or spoilt work.

Contents

Acknowledgements

I am grateful to the following companies and individuals who have given me their full support and cooperation throughout the preparation of this book.

Peter Ramsden, who designed and made most of the projects featured in this book, and without whose help, friendship and encouragement this book would never have been published.

Andrew Litchfield, who designed and made the Poet's Seat.

Roger Southee and Steve Orley of BPIB, who work tirelessly in promoting the Eastern Canadian Timber Industries.

Michael White of Trade Connect who supplied us with Eastern Canadian white Pine from Goodfellow Inc. and Eastern Canadian white Cedar timber and shingles (roof tiles) from Sovebec Inc. All these timbers are from the province of Québec.

Guy Rancourt of Sovebec.

Michael Stenton and Tony Hickey of Stanley Tools, for the supply of Jet cut saws, chisels and woodworking equipment.

Anthony Parker, Managing Director of Nettlefolds, for the supply of 'Supascrews' which formed the basis of fixing things together.

Ian Rowley of Humbrol, for the supply of water-resistant wood adhesives.

John Roberts of Bosch Power Tools, whose wonderful battery-powered screwdrivers made assembling the projects so much faster.

Victor Wheeler, who supplied us with Ronseal.

The publisher would like to thank the following for supplying the photographs for this book:
Garden Answers pp. 8, 9, 10, 14, 15; Marie O'Hara pp. 13, 65, 89, 103–4, 105–16, 120–24; *Practical Gardening* pp. 1, 3, 6, 7, 16, 26, 32, 36, 47, 55, 73, 81, 94, 100, 106, 112, 119; Peter Ramsden/Richard Blizzard p.20.

Introduction

Woodworkers and gardeners have a great deal in common – they are both creative and practical. Gardeners peruse the seed catalogues in January, and in their mind's eye enjoy the prospect of what they will begin to create in their gardens come the spring. Woodworkers leaf through the tool catalogues and they too dream of what they will create, if only they had the tools and a little more time. Both these groups of talented people enjoy the prospect of the possible this year – time allowing – and if all is not finished this year then there is always next year to look forward to.

Just as gardening, woodworking has its ways of going about things; its dos and don'ts. The purpose of this book is to help and encourage those of my green-fingered friends who, given time and a set of sharp basic tools, can make some astounding things for a fraction of the cost of those commercially produced items they see in the garden centre. And as the woodworker makes garden projects he may also learn about such things as container plants needing drainage holes and climbing plants needing supports.

As with most things in life trying to run before you walk can damage your health! So before you start work on some tremendous wooden structure that may end up looking like a roof-rack for a camel try something a little more basic – learn the simple techniques from which you will be able to go forward with great success. So often projects are spoilt by being rushed into, so give yourself time and space. Study the plan you intend to work from –

identify where all the pieces go and then make a list of everything you need. Work out the lengths of wood you will need to cut from, and don't forget screws, glue and brushes for the wood preservative. When you get back home don't start cutting into your timber before carefully measuring everything, and don't cut anything until you have measured twice – timber is too precious to waste on avoidable mistakes.

Timber is a beautiful material, and it goes on 'living' after felling and seasoning. Even the oldest wooden beams removed from a 500 year-old house will still move! I like to think that the tree just takes on a different form of beauty; old chairs, rocking cradles, and wooden floors, if cared for, are a joy to look at. Wood is friendly to work with, its texture is gentle and like other material from growing things it rewards those who look after it and tend it. So get a feel for the material you are about to use, don't think of it as any old chunk of wood waiting for a big six-inch nail, but as the product of years of growing of a beautiful tree, from which you now have the pleasure of creating what you will – a new object of beauty.

Woodworkers and gardeners often reflect on what they have done in the past and what they intend to achieve in the future. I look back over the many books I have written, and projects I have created, and from these feel continually challenged to do better. The skills I have learned from one job get passed to the next. Design, style and construction methods all come under scrutiny. So, if you have that dreaded feeling that

ABOVE: Wall Plant Stand (see page 32).
OPPOSITE: Poet's Seat (see page 106).

something called a mortice and tenon is going to turn up like some perennial weed have no fear – in this book joints are out, but fixing pieces of timber together securely is very definitely in. New glues, screws and tools have come to the aid of all practical minded people. You don't have to be a budding cabinet-maker to enjoy this book. If you can measure accurately, cut along a line (yes, you will need a sharp saw – not one used to prop the greenhouse door open last summer) and apply wood preservative with a brush, then you are just about to get the woodworking bug! (Or is that a taboo word for garden projects?)

I hope the projects you make by using this book will add a new dimension to your garden, and that from the skills learned you will go on to design your own items.

Tools

Good hand and power tools are an investment, and I would strongly recommend that you buy from a brand leader: A hammer, for example, can be a dangerous tool, but if you buy a Stanley hammer you are assured of safety because the head of the hammer has been X-rayed to look for hair-line cracks in the 'casing'. Cheap hammer heads have been known to shatter and cause injury to the woodworker. Good tools – hammers, chisels, planes and saws – will last a lifetime so they are always a wise investment.

Saw

Despite the legend that grandad's old saw was the best ever made, don't believe it. Saw technology has gone a very long way since grandad had his saw and even he would have to acknowledge that the new jet-cut saws are astounding. Basically the tooth of the saw is sharpened in such a way that it is capable of cutting on both the up and down stroke. The teeth are 'case hardened', which means that they stay sharp for a very, very long time. Cutting a piece of wood will never be a problem again with one of the jet-cuts. The saws are produced in both hand- and tenon-saw form, and are very desirable acquisitions for anyone wanting to cut timber with little effort.

Rules, measuring tapes and set squares

These essential 'setting-out' tools are all necessary. I still like an old steel rule for all the small accurate marking out. However, the large expanding-type rule (these are the ones that wind themselves back into a case) are essential for working on the larger lengths of timber. Various sizes of

carpenter's square are available – don't buy an expensive one – and all steel is best. For marking out accurately it's another must.

Smoothing tools

The traditional Stanley plane is a beautiful tool and ideal for our projects, but there are alternatives. There is a plane with disposable blades, which is less expensive, and if you don't like oilstoning the traditional blade, then the disposable blade is a good alternative.

Surform planes come in many shapes and are excellent for rapid smoothing of sawn timber. The blade of the plane is a metal plate that has dozens of tiny blades across its surface, and it removes wood fibres in the same way as a cheese grater removes cheese. Take a look at what is available before you buy a plane.

ABOVE: From both an investment and a safety point of view, it is worth buying good-quality tools.

Drills, bradawls, screwdrivers and screws

Anyone who has ever tried to drive a screw into a piece of timber without a pilot hole will know that it is difficult, and more than likely the head of the screw becomes damaged in the process and yes, you do get blisters in the palm of your hand! The wood-bit (always called a drill) has to be used first to bore a hole. Ideally the hole should be the diameter of the screw's steel shank, so that when the screw goes into the wood it is the threaded portions that force themselves into the wood fibres. The screw head has a number of shapes – countersunk being the most popular, and in garden fixings the raised head (rounded on top) black-painted screw is also very popular. For the ordinary countersink screw a countersink bit is necessary after the hole has been bored. This countersink hole in the wood allows the head of the screw to lie flush with the surface of the timber.

New screw technology has come along to make some tasks easier. The head of the screw is no longer a slot – remember how the screwdriver used to slip out and damage the work. The cross head has remedied this, allowing an easier screw driving to take place; the threads of the modern screw are coarser in pitch; and the screws are usually zinc-plated – a must for outdoor structures. Nettlefolds Supascrews have all these features, and are perfect fixing devices for all things wooden. The technique to be used for fixing timber together with screws is to bore a pilot hole; use a countersink bit to give an indentation for the screw head; then drive the screw home.

The bradawl is one of those tools that are used all the time, but because they are so simple tend to get forgotten. The bradawl looks like a small screwdriver with a shaped end. Its purpose is to mark the position for a screw, to 'get a start' in the wood, by making a hole.

Screwdrivers must be one of the most misused tools in the workshop. They tend to be used for things that they were never designed for such as scraping and levering lids off paint tins. A number of different sized screwdrivers is a must, and if you are buying new ones then look out for Magnum as these have a cushioned handle and are the safest and most comfortable screwdrivers that I have ever come across.

Drill bits need to be kept sharp, and for this purpose many fairly inexpensive devices are available. It is well worth the effort to keep the drill bit sharp as it relieves frustration and spoiled work. Don't ever be tempted to use your drill bits to drill into stone or concrete – for this job masonry drill bits are necessary.

Clamps and clamping devices

Accidents happen when the timber being worked slips. There are not short cuts to be taken here, you **must** clamp the timber firmly before working upon it.

The Black & Decker Workmate is a good investment for all kinds of D.I.Y. work. Not only has it a jaws clamping device, but on the later models one of the tables turns through 90 degrees and acts as a clamp, thus holding timber firmly on the Workmate table top.

In addition to the Workmate it is essential to have some additional clamps to hold the timber firmly to a solid working surface.

Chisels and mallets

A set of firm chisels, a mallet and an oilstone are absolute necessities for the tool box. The wooden mallet is the only tool that should ever be used to hit the end of a wooden chisel handle as it is the kindest tool to deliver such hard blows. I use it on the new plastic-handled chisels. Today, however, the new plastics are so hard that they will not split or shatter. Perhaps it is still the traditionalist in me that cannot strike a chisel handle with anything other than a wooden mallet.

Stanley Tools make a set of chisels that have four convenient sizes. They are known as the Handyman set and represent excellent value.

LEFT: To avoid accidents, make sure you clamp timber firmly before any work begins.

Power tools

Power tools get jobs done much quicker. Planing, sawing and sanding are some of the more labour intensive jobs that these machines can do for you. There are a number of manufacturers of these tools and all of them perform well. Today many of the traditional corded tools are cordless and battery-powered. Don't be fooled into thinking that the power is not there – battery technology has gone a long way in the last five years. There are some very real advantages with the battery tool, particularly for the gardener. You can use tools in the garden without trailing leads and, of course, there is no danger of electrocution.

Battery-powered screwdriver/drill

These tools are so useful that they are finding a home in most tool sheds. Two speeds allow for drilling and screwdriving. The torque, or clutch setting, allows the clutch to slip when the screw head has been fully driven home. A reverse is fitted to allow for the extraction of screws, and a slow start is included on most models. The slow start and the use of cross-head screws allow the woodworker/ gardener a hundred per cent success rate when driving screws into wood. Once you have used one of these machines you will wonder how you managed without one.

Jigsaw

The name is somewhat misleading as it suggests that it only cuts wooden puzzles. This machine is a very sophisticated cutting tool, the larger ones being able to cut mild steel plate. It is good to look for a jigsaw that has a small support wheel directly behind the blade. The little roller wheel gives

both blade and the piston arm that drives the blade, support. You can get jigsaws that have pendulum actions and a whole range of speeds. The variety of blades is amazing allowing this tool to cut wood, steel, plastics and even felt. It is perhaps the safest electrically powered saw as it cuts more slowly than other saws. The jigsaw is unique in that it is the only saw that can actually cut out circles and shapes from the middle of a piece of timber.

Circular saw

Hand-held circular saws have been around for a long time. They are wonderful for ripping down a long

ABOVE: A battery-powered screwdriver saves time, especially on larger projects.

plank, but they do need **great** care on the part of the operator. They are usually fitted with tungsten carbide teeth, and it is advisable to buy one that has such a blade. The reason being that the T.C.T. teeth blunt more slowly, and will cut man-made boards easily. **A note of caution**: watch your fingers as things can happen very quickly and if the blade binds in the wood, you can lose control of the machine. A blunt blade will tend to ride out of the timber being cut, and will obviously be difficult to control. Used with care and with the cutting timber clamped on the bench, they are excellent tools.

Planer

The hand-held planer is very useful if you intend planing up all your sawn timber. It has a circular cutter block that has two blades which rotate at high speed. Its cutting action is actually 'chipping off' particles of wood. Sawn timber is less expensive than planed, so the machine is a very good investment if you intend to do a great deal of timber planing. Some planes can cut rebates, and also have a useful guide device in the base of the machine that enables it to cut 45 degree mitres on the edge of planks.

Orbital sanders

Smoothing down timber, paint work, or wood preservative before the next application is always a tedious job. The orbital sander does this rapidly, and because it 'orbits' as it works it does not leave any scratches. You will also discover that a sheet of abrasive lasts a long time. The better orbital sanders come with a dust bag – which for me is an essential feature.

Finger sanders

These machines have a short arm around which runs a continuous belt of glass-paper. They are very useful for working around corners and smoothing down all sorts of intricate woodworking shapes. There is a certain knack to working with these machines, but this you will learn quite quickly.

Band-saw

A band-saw is a two-wheeled (in some cases three-wheeled) machine that has a continuous band of toothed steel blade around its wheels. The blade is held steady between the two wheels by a system of guides. Timber is placed upon the saw table and fed into the blade. The band-saw can cut almost any shape in timber. Different blades are available. For the home woodworker these machines are very useful and can speed up wood-cutting operations.

Pillar drill

It is frequently necessary to drill holes accurately in timber at exactly 90 degrees. To help you do this your power drill can be clamped into a drill stand. This enables you to control the accuracy of the hole-drilling task. The pillar stand has a handle that lowers the drill into the timber to bore the hole. Drills mounted on stands are very much more easily controlled.

Tool maintenance

Always clean your tools after use. I wipe mine over with a rag and/or spray oil. Don't store either hand or power tools in a damp garage. Ideally, make a tool box to take all your kit (allow extra space for additions) and put one of those small tubular electric heaters in the bottom (the type used for preventing pipes and tanks in lofts freezing); bore a hole in the top of the box to allow the heat to escape. The worst thing for any tool is to be left in a cold damp atmosphere and then taken into a warm shed. This causes condensation on the steel surface and leads to the formation of rust.

Safety

Use protective eye shields when working with tools – a stray shaving, or something breaking off can cause irreparable damage to the eyes. It is a good idea to buy half a dozen safety goggles and hang them in obvious places in the workshop. Even if you lose one there is always another pair to hand.

• Don't ever use a blunt tool. You will have to force a blunt tool to do its job, it will slip and both you and the tool will probably suffer damage. The rule applies to hand tools and power tools.

• Don't ignore the manufacturers' instructions. Familiarize yourself with the machine before using it. Don't rush into working with it.

• Don't let anyone talk to you or distract you while you work.

• Don't work when you are tired: discipline yourself to take another day to finish off.

• Don't answer the telephone – you put the job down, may come back distracted, and accidents and spoiled work will be the outcome.

• Don't lend your tools to someone else – it is likely to be the end of a good friendship.

• Make sure that the area you work in is clear of obstacles such as tools, pieces of wood on the floor, and cables to trip over.

• Ensure that your working surface is firm and use clamps on everything you drill, screw or saw.

• If you have big pieces of timber to cut make sure that you can complete the cut, that you won't get tangled with something, that the power tool cable is of sufficient length and that the machine is not 'strangled' halfway through the operation.

• If you work in your garage on these projects make certain that the car is out, and that you have sufficient light. Heating is also important as cold fingers cannot feel or grip well.

• Make sure that children cannot come in while machines are working.

• Be sure that all machines are off before you leave. Chisels, Stanley knives and most tools should all be stored well out of the reach of a child.

Materials

This is not a book for the skilled or even semi-skilled woodworker – it is for the beginner, and it is worth noting that in the past ten years five factors have altered the traditional way of constructing garden furniture: timber, glue, screws, wood preservatives and tool technology.

Timber

Timber is kind to work with, is readily available in many countries and with it you can make most things. It is the only sustainable raw material on the planet, and by being careful where you buy your timber, a totally renewable source can then be guaranteed.

In recent years we have become aware of the damage that has already been done to our planet by the wholesale extraction of natural resources such as minerals and timbers for solely profit-driven motivation. Massive areas of tropical forest, plants and animals have been lost forever in this decade alone. In some areas of the world the wholesale destruction continues, such as in Cambodia, where the felling and the clearance of hardwoods is a disaster. The consumer has to be knowledgeable about what, exactly, a sustainable source of timber is and know which countries have a re-afforestation and long-term planting strategy. Armed with this knowledge the customer should ask questions about the origins of the timber he or she is buying.

So, what can you buy, and where can you buy it? The Scandinavian countries have in place a long-term forestry programme. They are growing and planting more trees than they are cutting. To get some idea of just how much timber is growing, it has been calculated that in every 'growing hour' (trees grow more slowly in the winter) sufficient growth rings are added to the trees to build 12 wooden houses an hour. In 12 months sufficient timber is grown to build a row of houses from Barcelona to Helsinki! The felling of trees is carefully controlled and a strict code of practice is followed: not all the trees in the logging area are cut; and trees in rocky outcrops are left, as are large old pines to provide nesting places for eagles. If the nesting site of an eagle or osprey is discovered in the branches of a tree, then this tree and the ones around it are left in place. Old snags (broken trees) as habitats for wood-boring insects and woodpeckers; aspen, willow and mountain ash; small tree stumps; hardwood by the edges of brooks and streams that shade the watercourse; and large hardwood trees, conifers and low-growing vegetation by lake shores are all left uncut. After the activity of men and machines a very strict clean-up takes place to remove all environmentally damaging material such as empty diesel barrels, lubricants, old tyres and hoses. River courses and brooks are checked to see that machines have not blocked them. The forests are well managed and the environment cared for to protect the creatures that live there.

From these Scandinavian countries we get a readily available supply of pine such as Nordic redwood, and whitewood of full-size Christmas trees. The redwood is more easily worked and is used extensively in pine furniture. The whitewood is used mainly in house building for roof trusses and floorboards. Builders' merchants keep both these timbers in stock in a large variety of sizes. You can buy it 'off the shelf' in either its sawn state or planed. Buying sawn timber is cheaper, and in many ways this pre-planed state is far better for garden items, such as furniture and pergolas, than the planed variety because sawn timber produces a much better 'key' for the wood preservative to stick to. However, if you are making furniture such as a seat or a garden bench then it is necessary to plane up the planks you intend to sit on.

Buying timber

In some timber yards there seems to be a coded language, and unless you know exactly what you want, or don't know the jargon, they look at you as if you have two heads, big ears and fangs! So before you enter the yard, do have a rough cutting list prepared, and breeze in with the phrase 'Have you got any really dry whitewood boards? And I don't want the one with large pockets of resin'. That will do it – it's like cracking the secret code. Now be careful, if the timber offered feels wet, it probably is, so ask to see another shed. Today sawn timber comes in from the docks in large pre-wrapped packages, having been kiln-dried before leaving its country of origin, and good timber yards have it covered. It is also helpful to go with an expanding Stanley rule, and don't forget a pencil behind your ear. If you can avoid early Monday morning when the merchants' big-spending builders are in, so much the better – choose a time when the yard is not packed with 'jobbing' builders' trucks, and you will get better service. Sometimes you can get a 'job lot' of timber, so if you are intending to build trellises or just a decorative arch, then this could be a good buy.

Timber shapes

Besides the standard sizes of sawn and planed timber, you can buy a range of pre-formed timber such as

garden bench in Nordic whitewood will last many decades. It has to be considered that the cost of teak or iroko, for example, is much more expensive than Nordic whitewood.

Glues

Gone are the days when the carpenter had an old glue pot boiling on the stove – not only did it smell revolting, but, although water resistant, it was not waterproof. Water-resistant glue is usually adequate for most garden projects, but, if you decide to build a boat for the pond in your garden, for example, then you need waterproof glue which is necessary where immersion in water is envisaged all the time. But if you are going to build tables, benches or plant containers then water-resistant glue is all you really need.

Evostick make glues that are easily identifiable for interior or exterior use. The bottles of glue packed in green containers are suitable only for interior use; the glues packed in blue bottles are for outdoor use and are labelled as water resistant. The glue comes in user-friendly bottles – there is even a stopper to prevent the glue congealing and a dispenser spout.

However good your woodwork joints are, the use of glue is essential. In the constructions in this book screws are used, but glue and screws will give greater rigidity to the structure. It is also worth bearing in mind that glue sticks wood surfaces together better if the surfaces to be jointed are rough or keyed. If you have two nice pieces of smooth planed timber then use a knife where the joint is to be, and key it with the blade by cutting a criss-cross pattern on to the surface. If your joints are

planks and mouldings. Perhaps the most common is the ship-lap boarding used on garden sheds, but there are many others.

One of the most useful pre-formed timber boards is tongued and grooved board, and there are two types selected for some of the projects in this book. The tongued and grooved square-edge board, used for floor boards – the tongue of one board slips into the groove of the other to make it a strong joint – is ideal for the bottom of flower and display boxes. Decorative-edge 'V' tongued and grooved board is ideal for the sides of items such as boxes. The 'V' section on the side gives the board a decorative line and looks very pleasing. Once you have familiarized yourself with these two types of board a whole new concept of wooden containers is possible. Not only is this a particularly simple method of construction, the finished item looks very professional.

Most builders' merchants keep a stock of mouldings. These are pre-

shaped pieces of timber that are glued and panel-pinned in place – usually on to a large item of furniture to give it a particular look or style. You will need to experiment with these and find shapes and styles that you like. A moulding can make a simple, basic flower box very stylish, and by using different mouldings can give the same box a completely different look.

Timber colours

We have certainly become aware of the need to prevent the wholesale destruction of rain forests, and in looking for dark-coloured timber many home owners and D.I.Y. woodworkers have discovered water-based wood preservatives that give reach teak or mahogany colouring to Nordic pine wood. It has been a common misunderstanding that pine rots in the garden and tropical hardwoods never do. In fact all timber is deserving of some maintenance if it is to last, and if some preservative treatment is maintained a straight from the saw then there will be sufficient key for the glue to get the best possible adhesion.

Modern glues do not need massive amounts of pressure to get them to stick. I use lightweight clamps on my joints and find these more than adequate. The glue is stronger than the wood fibres it is holding together. Test this for yourself by glueing some offcuts together and try breaking the joint after the glue has set!

Screws

The new supascrews, made by Nettlefolds, are a great improvement and their larger, coarser thread even ensures a good hold in end-grain, something the old traditional screw could never do. The cross head means that you rarely get a slip when you start to drive a screw. Using the combination of these two fixing methods of screws and glue means not only a fail-proof joint, but also a more quickly made structure. The real skills are measuring accurately and cutting off the ends of timber squarely.

For the majority of projects in this book mainly No. 8 gauge screws were used in lengths varying from 3 cm (1¼ in) to 3.8 cm (1½ in). Other sizes required are listed in the projects.

The countersink zinc-plated screw was used a great deal. The zinc plating stops the screw rusting, which in turns prevents those ugly brown rusty marks discolouring the project. Coach bolts were used for fixing items of large dimensions that from time to time may need to be dismantled. Use zinc-plated bolts, other types will rust and this will prevent their removal.

Wood preservatives

Timber is a fairly durable substance. Some timbers will deteriorate faster

ABOVE: Modern preservatives allow the use of soft wood on many projects.

than others, and some have no resistance to the 'big outdoors' at all. Nordic redwoods and whitewoods are suitable for garden projects, the whitewood having a molecular structure that actually repels the water. Even timber not treated with a preservative, provided that it dries off naturally, will last quite a long time. However, you will want to preserve the timber projects you make for as long as possible. In the past the greatest mistake was to use ordinary paint or varnish, which trapped any moisture in the timber, and especially in the case of a varnish finish, the trapped moisture tended to discolour the wood.

The new quick drying wood stains have many advantages: they are microporous, allowing the wood to breathe; they resist cracking and peeling; the next coat can be applied in about four hours; they have very little odour; and the brush can be cleaned in water. I have found that these preservatives have lasted a full three years, keeping the timber completely sound, before further maintenance and re-coating is necessary before the winter. A wide variety of colours is available. I also find that this type of preservative is easy to apply, and forgiving – if you apply too much, brush it out and when it dries there is no sign of any runs or dribbles of preservative.

Techniques

I hope it is safe to assume you are not a carpenter or cabinetmaker. If you are then this section is not for you! However, if you are a practical type, and have never done any woodworking before then this tells you to put simple techniques to good use without losing your hair or temper. The processes described are common to all the projects.

Choosing and cutting timber

When you buy your timber make sure that it is not only dry to the feel, but cast your eye along the timbers and find the straightest pieces possible. If you are making legs avoid knots as much as possible, as they will form weak areas on the leg. Knots in planks are all right providing that they are firm (that is, they do not drop out like old pegs).

Before you start work clear your bench top and familiarize yourself with the cutting list you have made. If your project is a four-legged bench cut out all the legs together, so they are identical in length. Use a set square to mark across all the legs with a good clean pencil line, and as you use your saw to cut the timber to length, make certain that you cut at 90 degrees to the top. Cuts with untidy angles can be extremely difficult to fit if you have to butt one end up against another.

Simple jointing

Try to do all your marking out before you start any jointing (fixing wood together). Always measure twice. This prevents wastage. You also need to remember that in most things that there is a left- and right-hand side – a simple notion, that is often forgotten.

Once all the pieces of wood are cut to length identify each bundle and make a start by marking out where the pieces cross or join. You will need to do this using a set square and pencil. Mark clearly where the screws will go.

Before attempting to glue and screw anything together have a 'dry run'. Assemble all the pieces on a flat surface. Now think three-dimensionally. Can you see how the side joins the back and front? Are the rails in the right places? Are the spacings correct? If this piece of timber goes there, what happens next? Try to work out in your mind where all the pieces will fit.

When you have decided to do the assembly do not attempt to glue up the whole thing in one go. Take it in sections, for example glue the front frame together, and then the back frame. When the glue has dried the side rails can be applied easily. Old experienced woodworkers have got a knack of working by themselves and can do more with one pair of hands than most ordinary mortals. As a newcomer get some help: ask someone to hold the pieces for you to put them all together.

Use cramps to hold timber together until you can drive screws in to hold pieces firmly. Don't forget the glue!

Hiding the screws that hold the job together

You may like to hide screw heads as they can spoil the line of the furniture. You will need to buy a plug cutter and a matching drill countersink which are available as a pair, and you can drill both the pilot hole for the screw and the deep countersunk hole into which the screw head and the plug go. Use the plug cutter to cut the wooden plug, that is to be glued on top of the screw head, from the face side of a suitable waste piece of timber. The plug is glued and hammered into the hole,

over the screw. When the glue is dry, use a sharp chisel to cut off the waste part of the plug, leaving a very tidy, almost invisible plug. When the preservative is applied you will not be able to detect the joint. Don't try to economize by cutting dowel rod and filling the hole – it won't work because the grain does not match. The grain of the dowel is the end-grain, whereas the piece you are working on will be cross-grain (the plug cutter takes the plug from the face of the timber). When wood preservative is applied the end-grain would always show clearly through. So the countersink and plug cutter are a real investment.

I hope that having read this far, you will now be sufficiently inspired to have a go at one of the most simple and useful joints – the halving joint which allows jointed timber pieces to lie flush with one with the other. As the name suggests, the halving joint requires the cutting away of half the thickness of one piece of timber and an equivalent piece to be cut away in the other timber to be jointed. The tools required are a tenon saw, Stanley knife, rule, marking gauge, chisel, clamp, mallet, pencil and a set square.

Make a start by placing one piece of timber on the other. Use the set square and pencil to mark in the width of one timber on the other. Now set up the marking gauge by adjusting the wooden slider to allow the gauge spur point to half the thickness of the timber. The marking gauge spur is better to mark with than a pencil because when you come to use the tenon saw to cut, the saw blade tends to follow the spur line. The width of the timber is marked, and the thickness, so pencil in hatched lines to show what needs to be cut away – it is so easy to cut the wrong bit if you fail to do this.

Fix the timber finally to the bench

ABOVE: Modern glues and screws mean only the simplest of woodworking joints are needed.

and cut down the sides of the gauge lines with a tenon saw. Now using a chisel start to cut away the timber in the middle. Use the largest chisel possible. Don't attempt to cut it away all at once; work from the top angling the chisel slightly upwards. About halfway down turn the timber around, and work from the other side. The last few cuts need to be made with the chisel on the marking gauge spur line. You will find that the timber between the two saw cuts crumbles out as you use the chisel – this is because you are working across the grain. It is far easier to do than to describe. The same has to be done on the other piece of timber, removing half of its thickness.

Once the joints have been cut on both pieces of timber, assemble your halving joint. If it will not fit together nicely – aim for a push fit – you can easily see where a little more timber has to be chiselled off. If the joint is a very loose fit, don't despair as modern glues are gap filling so all is not lost. Of all the woodworking joints this is perhaps the simplest and yet most useful to learn. In a spare moment practise the joint on a scrap piece of wood.

Richard Blizzard

Mosaic Herb Planters

These small square and triangular shaped planters were designed to be used in groups to form borders around corners or islands of plants. The two shapes allow you to produce many different design layouts, see figure 1.1. The planters can be used out in the open, or against a building or wall. If you chock up the central ones you can make three-dimensional structures such as pyramids.

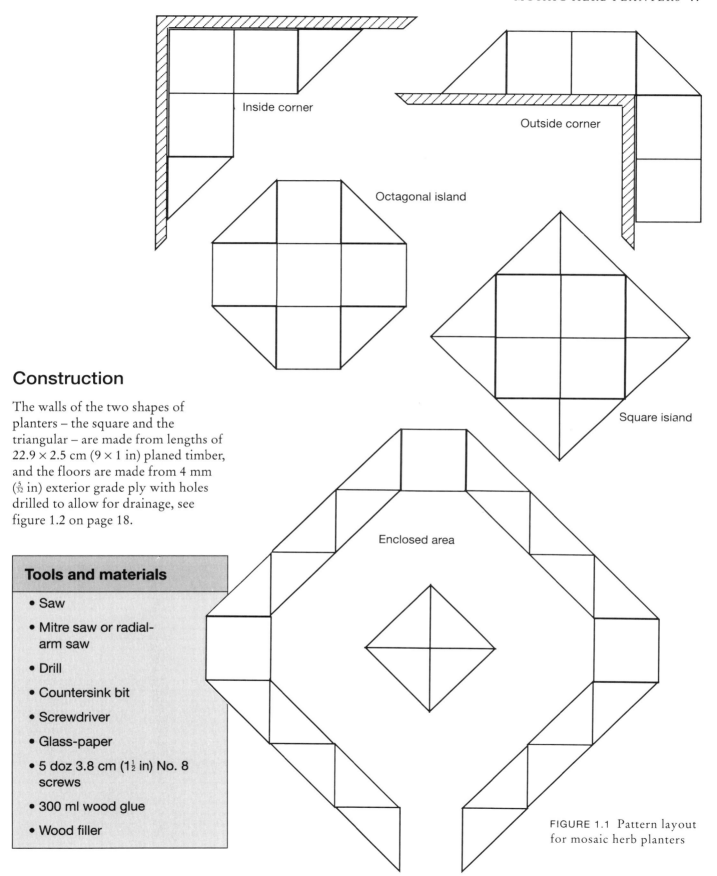

Inside corner

Outside corner

Octagonal island

Square island

Enclosed area

FIGURE 1.1 Pattern layout
for mosaic herb planters

Construction

The walls of the two shapes of
planters – the square and the
triangular – are made from lengths of
22.9 × 2.5 cm (9 × 1 in) planed timber,
and the floors are made from 4 mm
($\frac{5}{32}$ in) exterior grade ply with holes
drilled to allow for drainage, see
figure 1.2 on page 18.

Tools and materials

- Saw

- Mitre saw or radial-
arm saw

- Drill

- Countersink bit

- Screwdriver

- Glass-paper

- 5 doz 3.8 cm (1$\frac{1}{2}$ in) No. 8
screws

- 300 ml wood glue

- Wood filler

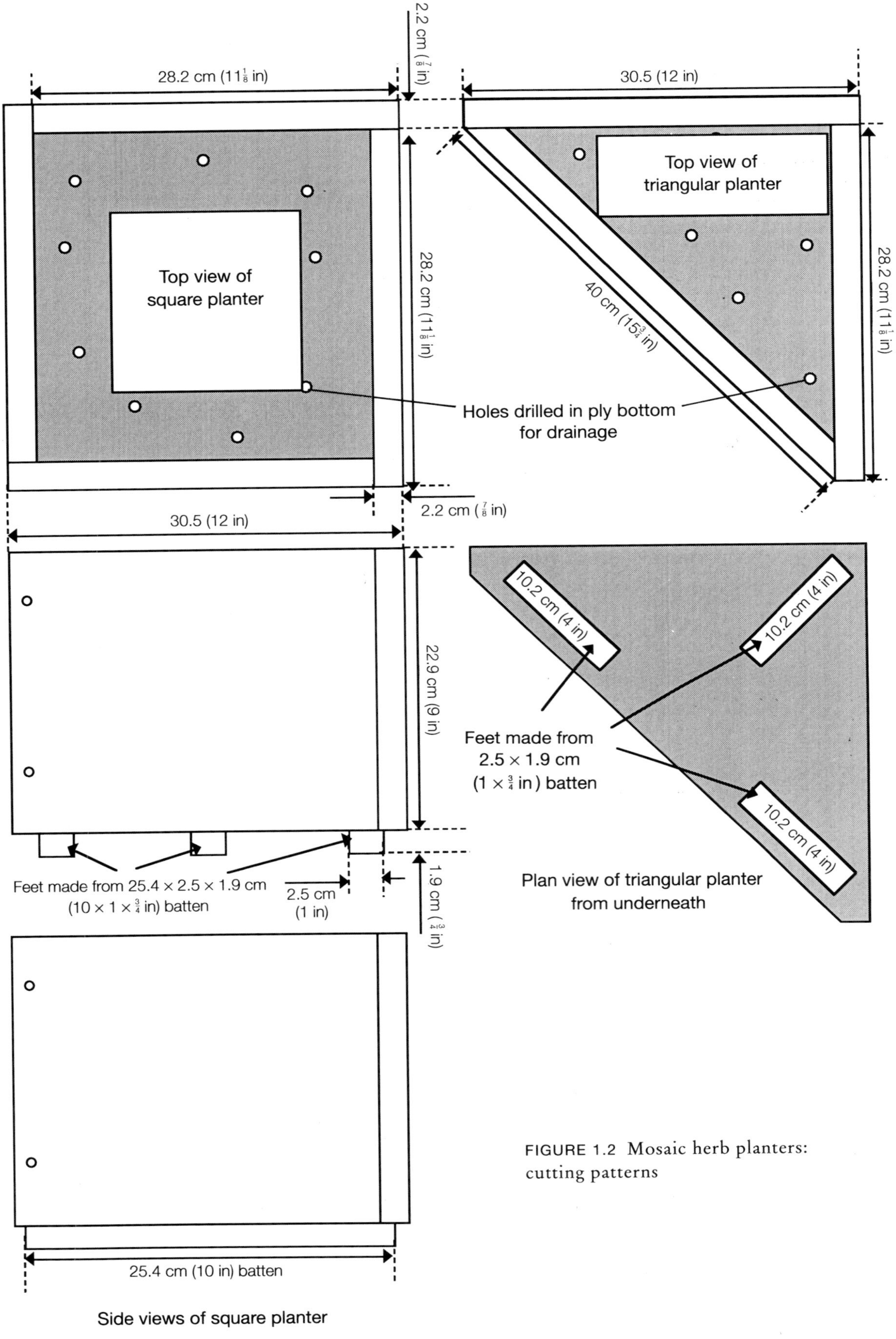

2.2 cm ($\frac{7}{8}$ in)

28.2 cm (11$\frac{1}{8}$ in)

30.5 (12 in)

Top view of
square planter

Top view of
triangular planter

28.2 cm (11$\frac{1}{8}$ in)

28.2 cm (11$\frac{1}{8}$ in)

40 cm (15$\frac{3}{4}$ in)

Holes drilled in ply bottom
for drainage

2.2 cm ($\frac{7}{8}$ in)

30.5 (12 in)

22.9 cm (9 in)

10.2 cm (4 in)

10.2 cm (4 in)

10.2 cm (4 in)

Feet made from
2.5 × 1.9 cm
(1 × $\frac{3}{4}$ in) batten

Plan view of triangular planter
from underneath

Feet made from 25.4 × 2.5 × 1.9 cm
(10 × 1 × $\frac{3}{4}$ in) batten

2.5 cm
(1 in)

1.9 cm ($\frac{3}{4}$ in)

25.4 cm (10 in) batten

Side views of square planter

FIGURE 1.2 Mosaic herb planters:
cutting patterns

Timber cutting list (Square planter)

Part	Quantity	Dimensions (L × W × Th)
Walls	4 (Planed timber)	28.2 × 22.9 × 2.5 cm $11\frac{1}{8}$ × 9 × 1 in
Feet	3 (Battening)	25.4 × 2.5 × 1.9 cm 10 × 1 × $\frac{3}{4}$ in
Floor	1 (4 mm ($\frac{5}{32}$ in) ply)	30.5 × 30.5 × 4 mm 12 × 12 × $\frac{5}{32}$ in

Timber cutting list (Triangular planter)

Part	Quantity	Dimensions (L × W × Th)
Wall	1 (Planed timber)	28.2 × 22.9 × 2.5 cm $11\frac{1}{8}$ × 9 × 1 in
Wall	1 (Planed timber)	30.5 × 22.9 × 2.5 cm 12 × 9 × 1 in
Wall	1 (Planed timber)	40 × 22.9 × 2.5 cm $15\frac{3}{4}$ × 9 × 1 in with 45 degree angled ends
Feet	3 (Battening)	10.2 × 2.5 × 1.9 cm 4 × 1 × $\frac{3}{4}$ in
Floor	1 (4 mm ($\frac{5}{32}$ in) ply)	30.5 × 30.5 × 40 cm 12 × 12 × $15\frac{3}{4}$ in

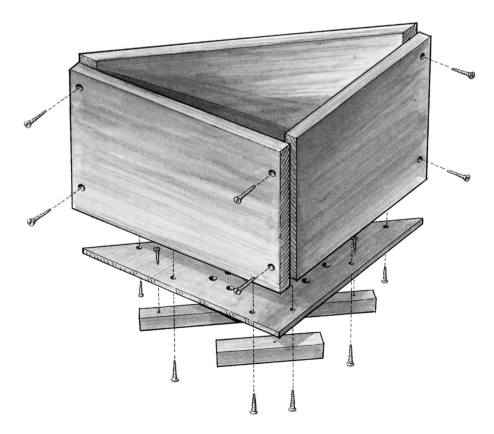

Square planter

1 Assemble the four walls by butting each end up against the end of the next wall, so that when they are all assembled they form a square with 30.5 cm (12 in) sides. Remember that 22.9 × 2.5 cm (9 × 1 in) timber when planed actually measures 22.5 × 2.2 cm ($8\frac{7}{8}$ × $\frac{7}{8}$ in).

2 Glue and screw the walls together through each wall into the end of the next wall.

3 Screw and glue a 30.5 cm (12 in) square piece of ply on to the bottom to form a floor. Drill 0.6 cm ($\frac{1}{4}$ in) through the floor for drainage.

4 Then screw and glue the three lengths of batten to the underside of the floor to form the feet.

Triangular planter

1 Butt join the 30.5 cm (12 in) length and the 28.2 cm ($11\frac{1}{8}$ in) length at right-angles to form the two 30.5 cm (12 in) sides.

2 The 40 cm ($15\frac{3}{4}$ in) must have its ends cut at 45 degrees to form the third side of the triangle. Keeping these angles constant is difficult. You can use a radial-arm saw canted to 45 degrees and cut across the 22.9 cm (9 in) width with the timber flat on the bench. Alternatively use a mitre saw or make up a 22.9 cm (9 in) deep mitre box, to cut vertically down the 22.9 cm (9 in) width at 45 degrees to the length.

3 Place a triangular piece of ply on the base for the floor. Drill 0.6 cm ($\frac{1}{4}$ in) holes through the floor for drainage.

4 Screw and glue three lengths of batten to the base for the feet.

Jardinière

This neat plant stand can be used to form a small indoor potted garden on, or out of doors as a plant display stand – perhaps on the side of a patio.

Construction

The jardinière has four legs, a narrow top rail and wider middle and bottom rails made of planed timber (see figure 2.1). The legs can be shaped at the top either with sharp triangular points, or with a more domed pyramid. If you decide to shape the tops of the legs you will need to draw the shape on yourself and cut it with a tenon or coping saw.

All the rails are set into the legs giving a flush finish. To achieve this you have to cut rebates for the rails into the legs, and since they need to fit precisely, you need to cut accurately. Ideally you end up with a rebate that the rail can be forced into with a bit of a thump, so it's best to cut the rebates slightly too small (1 mm ($\frac{1}{32}$ in) or so), so that you can pare them out with a chisel to get an exact fit. If you are uncertain, try

practising on some spare bits of wood. You will find after a couple of tries that you are getting it right!

Thin laths, bent to shape, in the gap between the top rail and the middle rail on the long sides of the jardinière add an extra dimension to the look of the structure, and look particularly attractive if they are a different colour from the frame.

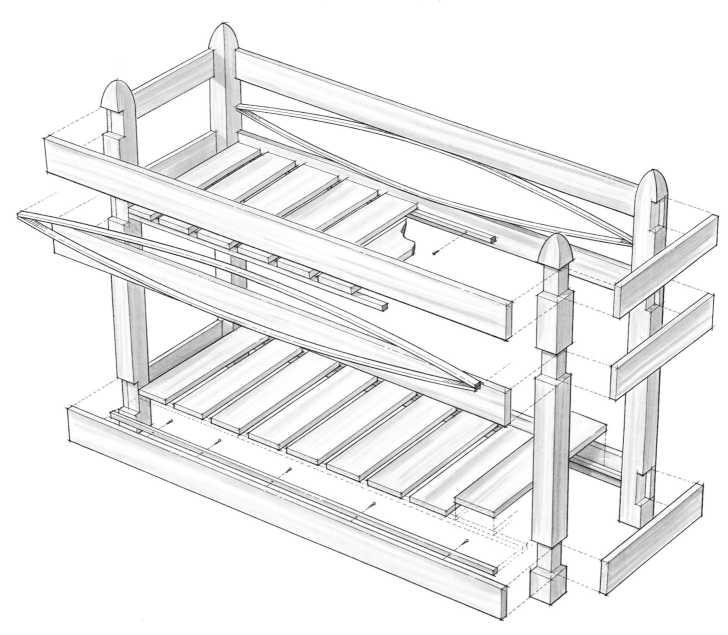

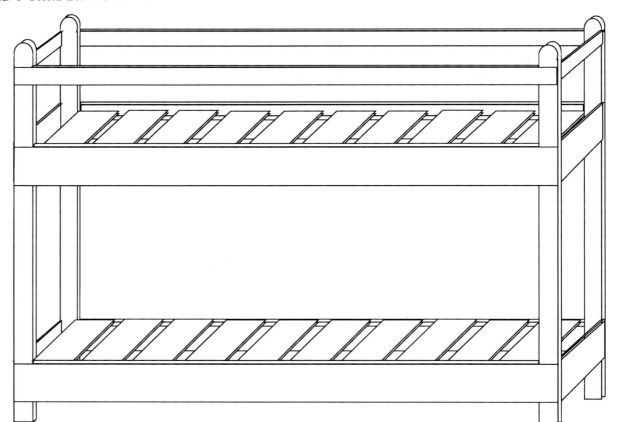

FIGURE 2.1
Jardinière

Tools and materials

- Tenon saw
- Coping saw
- Pencil
- Sticky tape
- Drill
- Screwdriver
- Glass-paper
- 'G' clamps
- Chisel
- Mallet
- Stanley knife
- 5 doz 4.4 cm (1¾ in) No. 8 screws
- 300 ml wood glue
- Paint or wood stain

Timber cutting list

Part	Quantity	Dimensions (L × W × Th)
Legs (shaped at top if required)	4 (Planed timber)	96.5 × 4.4 × 4.4 cm 38 × 1¾ × 1¾ in
Long top rails	2 (Planed timber)	122 × 4.4 × 1.6 cm 48 × 1¾ × ⅝ in
Short top rails	2 (Planed timber)	38.1 × 4.4 × 1.6 cm 15 × 1¾ × ⅝ in
Long rails	4 (Planed timber)	122 × 9.5 × 1.6 cm 48 × 3¾ × ⅝ in
Short rails	4 (Planed timber)	38.1 × 9.5 × 1.6 cm 15 × 3¾ × ⅝ in
Shelf supports	4 (Battening)	113 × 2.5 × 1.9 cm 44½ × 1 × ¾ in
Shelf slats	20 (Planed timber)	38.1 × 9.5 × 1.6 cm 15 × 3¾ × ⅝ in
Curved tracery	4 (Laths)	136 × 1.6 × 0.6 cm 54 × ⅝ × ¼ in

Cutting the rebates

1 First cut all the timber to length as in the cutting list.

2 Lay two legs side by side and place the next two on top. Line the ends up and tape them together, and draw a line with a rule all the way around the outside of the four legs as shown in figure 2.2a. This marks the sides that are going to have the rebates cut in them.

3 Take the tape off and lay all the legs out on a flat surface side by side with one pencil-marked side uppermost. Clamp or tape them together having made sure the tops and bottoms line up. Marking them up all together like this is the easiest way to get the rebates on all the legs at the same level. Place a short top rail on the legs at the correct level (see figure 2.2b). Use a set square to make sure it is at right-angles to the legs and, using the rail as a ruler, mark across the legs in pencil above and below the rail. Keep your pencil mark as tight into the rail as you can, so that when you cut the rebate out, the rail will fit tightly into it.

4 Mark the position for the middle and lower rails (remember the 9.5 cm ($3\frac{3}{4}$ in) planed timber instead of 4.4 cm ($1\frac{1}{4}$ in) as a ruler).

5 To get really sharp edges you should then scribe over all your lines with a Stanley knife, which gives a definite start for your saw, and leaves a fine edge.

6 Now untape and turn the legs so that the other pencilled sides are showing, and mark up the rebates in the same way on the other sides.

7 The next thing to do is to mark the depth of the rebate on the sides of the legs, so that you know how deep to cut into the leg. The easiest way to do this is to place a rail on end where it will eventually fit and draw round it on to the side of the leg (see figure 2.2c). Again make sure you keep your pencil marks in close to the rail end so that the fit will be tight.

8 To cut out the rebates it is best to do one first and check to see the rail fits tightly. Cut the wood down the lines to the depth marked, and then chisel out the wood. The neatest

way to do this is to take it out in small chunks, rather than trying to take the whole depth out at one go. When you get down close to the depth mark, work in from both sides towards the middle to avoid splitting the wood on the far side as you chisel it out.

9 Complete all the other rebates on the legs.

Glueing up the frame

1 You need a large flat surface on which you can work. First assemble one long side of the frame dry (i.e. without any glue). Check that the frame is square by checking that the diagonals of the rectangular space between the lower and the middle rails are equal.

2 When you have it all fitting nicely, take it apart and apply your wood glue.

3 Reassemble, check the diagonal again, and apply pressure to the joints using clamps or weights. Leave to set. Assemble the other long side in the same way.

4 When both are set, assemble the whole structure by fitting the short side rails. It is often easiest to do all this while standing the whole structure on a flat floor. Check that all the parts fit together properly and take apart for glueing.

5 Glue up and assemble. Remember to check the diagonals on the short sides for squareness. 'G' clamps are a great help in holding it all together while you work and while the glue sets.

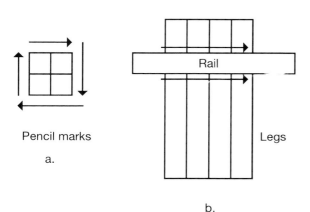

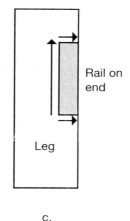

Pencil marks

a.

Rail

Legs

b.

Rail on end

Leg

c.

FIGURE 2.2 Marking the rebates

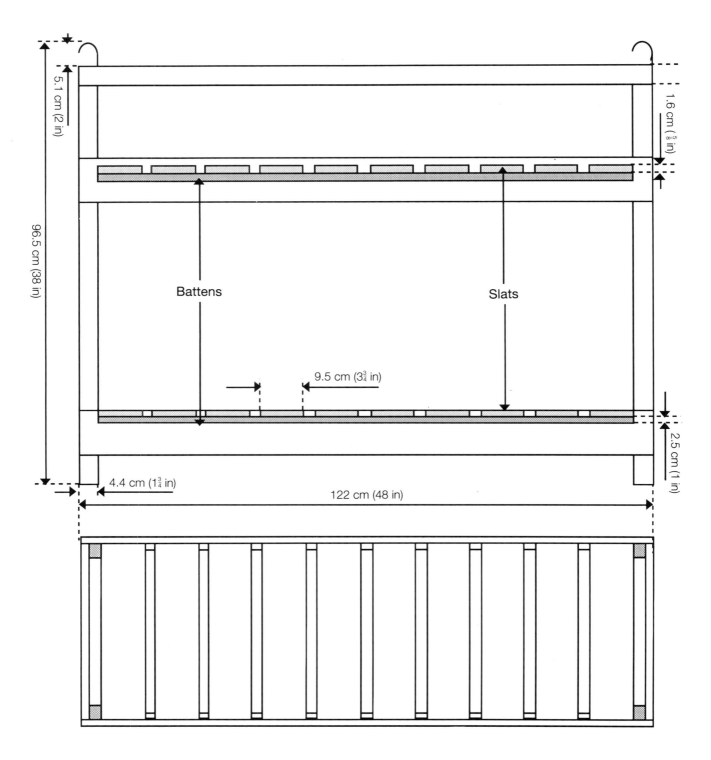

FIGURE 2.3 Jardinière cutting patterns

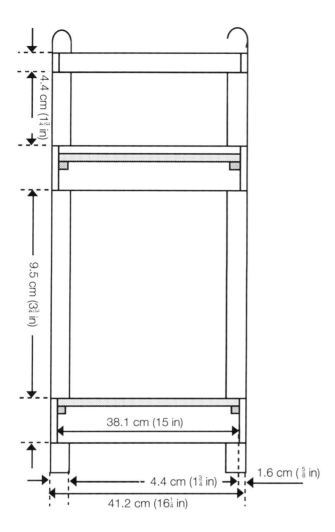

4.4 cm (1¾ in)

9.5 cm (3¾ in)

38.1 cm (15 in)

4.4 cm (1¾ in)

1.6 cm (⅝ in)

41.2 cm (16¼ in)

Shelves

1 Mark the positions of the battens, one on the inside of each long side of the middle and bottom rails. The battens for the top shelf are positioned so that the tops of the slats are recessed down a little from the top of the rail (see figures 2.1 and 2.3); and the battens for the bottom shelf so that the slats are flush with the top of the rails. Screw and glue the battens into position.

2 You will probably find it easiest to treat your jardinière before fitting the shelf slats. This way you can treat all the slats together on the flat, turn them, and get to the edges easily. It also makes the frame easier to treat. It does however mean that you will find it more difficult to use glue to fix the slats in as the glue does not get a firm fix on the preserved surface. If necessary use a Stanley knife to score the two surfaces to be joined to give the glue a key.

3 The shelf slats are all of the same length, with ten slats to each of the shelves. The slats can be fixed with pins or screws and glue (see step 2) and are spread out ten to a shelf with even spaces between each slat.

Tracery

1 Bend a length of thin lath into position, and mark the length with a pencil. The ends of the lath should be slightly at an angle so that it fits flush against the leg at each end.

2 The laths can be pinned or glued in place. It looks good if you have the laths a different colour from the frame.

Victorian Cloche

This design for a cloche is based on those used in Victorian gardens. It adds style to a utility item and looks good wherever it sits in your garden.

Tools and materials

- Pencil
- Flexible rule
- Circular saw or hand saw
- Drill
- Countersink bit
- Screwdriver
- Chisel
- Set square
- Flexible rule
- Paint or preservative
- 5 doz 3.8 cm (1½ in) No. 8 screws
- 300 ml pack waterproof glue

Timber cutting list

Part	Quantity	Dimensions (L × W × Th)
Frame end and side uprights	10 (Planed batten)	26.7 × 2.5 × 1.9 cm 10½ × 1 × ¾ in
Frame end outer uprights	4 (Planed batten)	30.5 × 2.5 × 1.9 cm 12 × 1 × ¾ in
Roof and side frame horizontals	10 (Planed batten)	61 × 2.5 × 1.9 cm 24 × 1 × ¾ in
Roof frame members	8 (Planed batten)	31.8 × 2.5 × 1.9 cm 12½ × 1 × ¾ in
End horizontals	4 (Planed batten)	41.9 × 2.5 × 1.9 cm 16½ × 1 × ¾ in
Roof moulding	1 (Moulding)	61 × 3.8 × 3.8 cm 24 × 1½ × 1½ in
End trim	1 (Timber)	54.6 × 2.5 × 1.3 cm 21½ × 1 × ½ in
End top trim	1 (Timber)	7.6 × 7.6 × 1.3 cm 3 × 3 × ½ in
Trims to fit over joins on both ends	lath or moulding	2.4 m × 2.5 cm 8 ft × 1 in for cutting to length
Side walls	2 (Acrylic sheeting)	61 × 30.5 cm 24 × 12 in
Roof panels	2 (Acrylic sheeting)	61 × 35.6 cm 24 × 14 in
End walls	2 (Acrylic sheeting)	45.7 × 30.5 cm 18 × 12 in
End gables	2 (Acrylic sheeting)	34.9 × 34.9 × 48.9 cm 13¾ × 13¾ × 19¼ in

Construction

The cloche frame, made from planed batten, is built around the acrylic sheets that form its windows (see figures 3.1 and 3.2). There are various types of clear plastic sheeting available but if you want the cloche to survive the summer sun, you need to use clear 2 mm (³⁄₃₂ in) acrylic sheeting.

Panels

1 The first job is to cut the acrylic sheeting wall and roof panels to size and shape. If you buy the sheeting at a builders' merchant, it is probably best to get the supplier to cut it to size for you. You can cut it with a circular saw or a hand saw, but it cracks easily.

Frame

1 Next cut the battening for the frame to length. The frame goes around the edge of the plastic sheets, and also partitions them up into smaller windows. Paint or treat all the battens before assembling, otherwise you will have to take it all to bits to paint it properly.

2 Fix the batten on to the sheets using countersunk screws. To do this you will need to drill holes of the correct size for the screws you are using, round the edges of the sheets. When drilling you need to have the sheet flat on a wood surface so that you can drill through and into some wood underneath, if you don't the acrylic will crack! You will need to countersink each hole. Four screws along the longer lengths and three along the shorter ones should be enough. Once the battens are screwed on to the sheets, you will find them much stiffer and more robust.

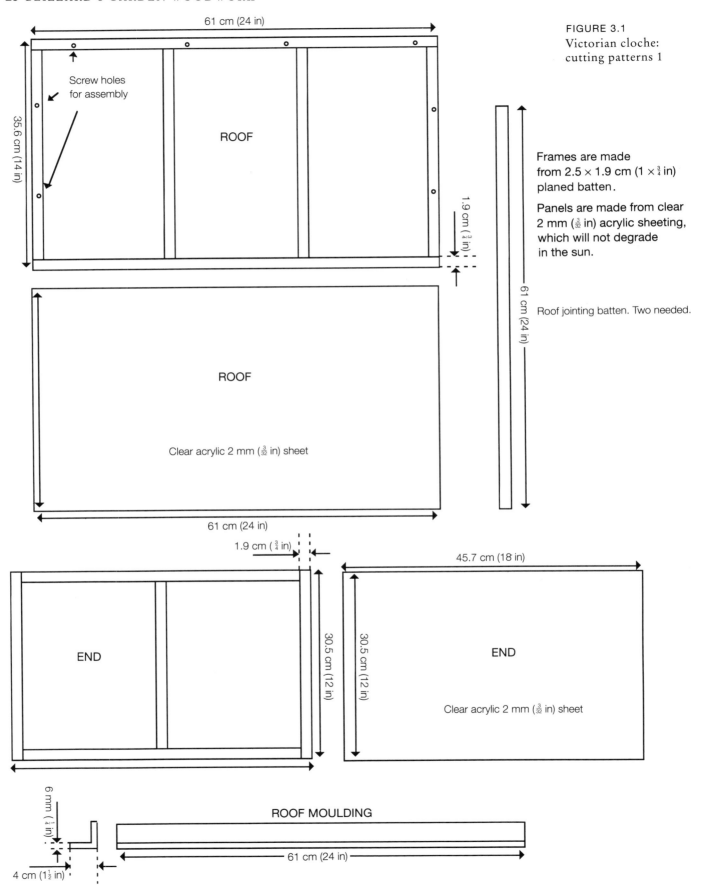

61 cm (24 in)

Screw holes
for assembly

ROOF

35.6 cm (14 in)

1.9 cm (³⁄₄ in)

FIGURE 3.1
Victorian cloche:
cutting patterns 1

Frames are made
from 2.5 × 1.9 cm (1 × ¾ in)
planed batten.

Panels are made from clear
2 mm (³⁄₃₂ in) acrylic sheeting,
which will not degrade
in the sun.

61 cm (24 in)

Roof jointing batten. Two needed.

ROOF

Clear acrylic 2 mm (³⁄₃₂ in) sheet

61 cm (24 in)

1.9 cm (³⁄₄ in)

45.7 cm (18 in)

END

30.5 cm (12 in)

30.5 cm (12 in)

END

Clear acrylic 2 mm (³⁄₃₂ in) sheet

6 mm (¼ in)

ROOF MOULDING

4 cm (1½ in)

61 cm (24 in)

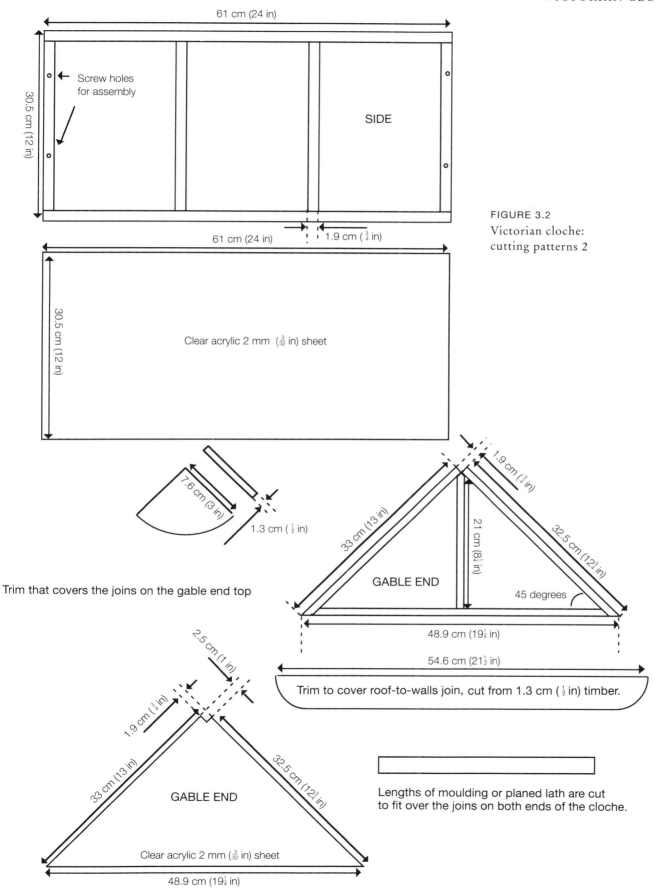

61 cm (24 in)

30.5 cm (12 in)

Screw holes for assembly

SIDE

61 cm (24 in)

1.9 cm ($\frac{3}{4}$ in)

FIGURE 3.2
Victorian cloche:
cutting patterns 2

30.5 cm (12 in)

Clear acrylic 2 mm ($\frac{3}{32}$ in) sheet

7.6 cm (3 in)

1.3 cm ($\frac{1}{2}$ in)

Trim that covers the joins on the gable end top

1.9 cm ($\frac{3}{4}$ in)

33 cm (13 in)

21 cm ($8\frac{1}{4}$ in)

32.5 cm ($12\frac{3}{4}$ in)

GABLE END

45 degrees

48.9 cm ($19\frac{1}{4}$ in)

54.6 cm ($21\frac{1}{2}$ in)

Trim to cover roof-to-walls join, cut from 1.3 cm ($\frac{1}{2}$ in) timber.

2.5 cm (1 in)

1.9 cm ($\frac{3}{4}$ in)

33 cm (13 in)

32.5 cm ($12\frac{3}{4}$ in)

GABLE END

Lengths of moulding or planed lath are cut
to fit over the joins on both ends of the cloche.

Clear acrylic 2 mm ($\frac{3}{32}$ in) sheet

48.9 cm ($19\frac{1}{4}$ in)

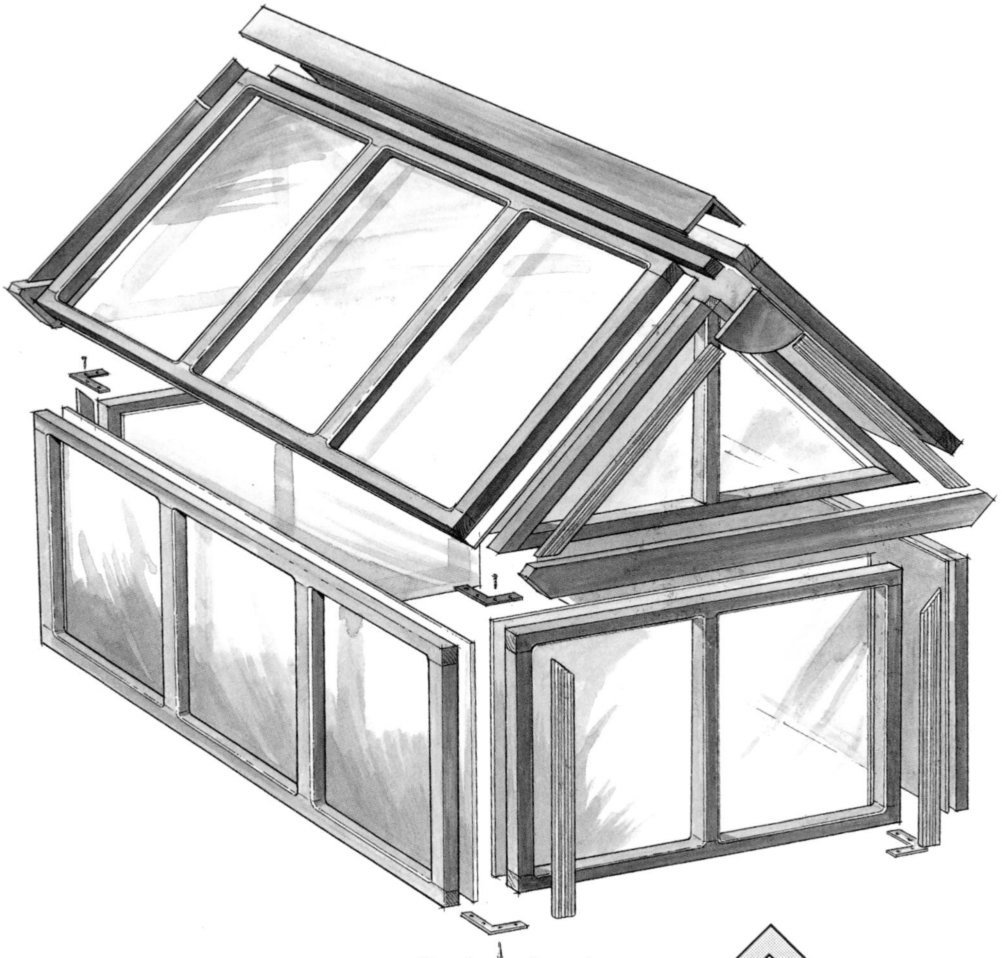

Walls

1 Use flat angled brackets to hold the four walls together, top and bottom. Fit the short end walls inside the long walls, with the plastic sheet on the inside. Check the diagonals from corner to corner to see that the structure is squared off.

2 To give the walls extra strength add two extra screws in both end vertical battens of the long walls. To do this drill through the batten and the plastic, countersink the hole in the wood and screw through both into the vertical end batten of the shorter wall.

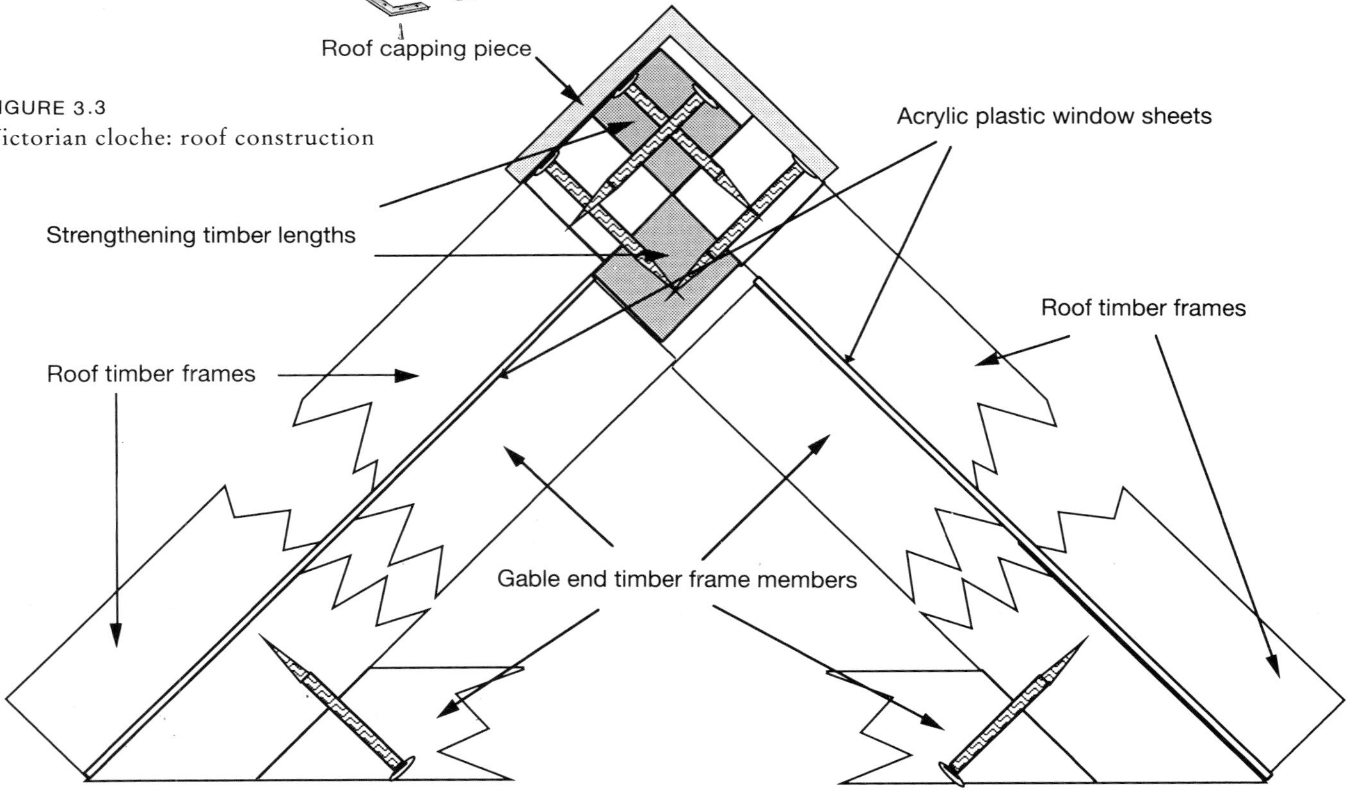

Roof capping piece

FIGURE 3.3
Victorian cloche: roof construction

Acrylic plastic window sheets

Strengthening timber lengths

Roof timber frames

Roof timber frames

Gable end timber frame members

Roof

1 To construct the roof you need to screw a length of batten to the long edge of one of the roof sections. Drill and then countersink four holes spaced out evenly along the long edge and then screw through into the length of batten.

2 Repeat the drilling process with the other roof piece, and screw that on to the same length of batten, so the two pieces are at right angles. This leaves a 'V' along the top. Then drill and screw another length of batten into the 'V'.

3 The end gable pieces are then fitted in at each end. Remember that the plastic should be on the inside. Drill a couple of holes through the wood and plastic of the end battens of the roof pieces and then screw through into the battens of the gable end.

4 Fit and glue the roof capping moulding into place and fit the circular quadrant over the ends. These can be screwed into place or tacked and glued.

5 Cut the roof-to-wall-join trim to shape and fix on to the horizontal batten of the gable ends. The top surfaces of the trim and the horizontal batten should be flush with one another. The roof will now be a very strong and sturdy structure, which fits down on to the body of the cloche, with the join trims holding it in position. If you don't want the roof to be removable you can screw through the trim into the top batten of the wall.

6 Finally, measure up and cut laths to trim and cover all the wood-plastic-wood sandwiches on the end walls and gables.

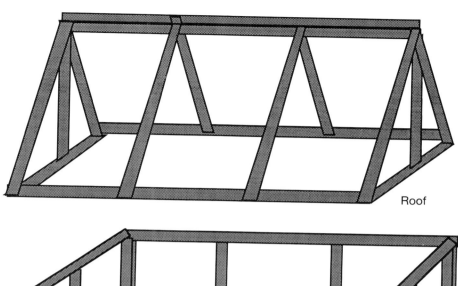

Roof

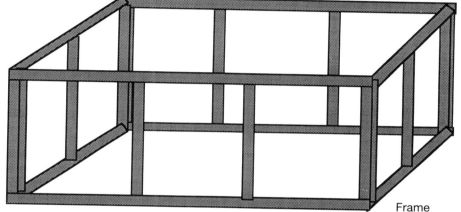

Frame

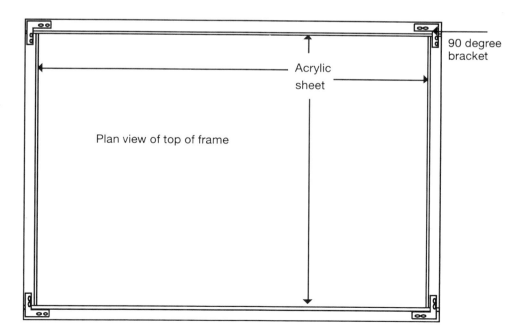

90 degree bracket

Acrylic sheet

Plan view of top of frame

FIGURE 3.4 Victorian cloche

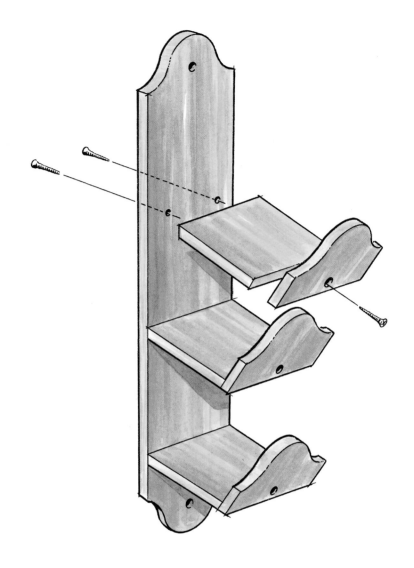

Wall Plant Stand

This useful set of wall stands allows you to display your potted plants, and at the same time decorate an empty wall. The stands tilt the plants slightly forward for easier watering.

Construction

The stands are made from planed timber and are basically very simple to make. There are, however, two tricky bits to watch for. The curves cut on the ends (see figure 4.1) can be easily cut using an electric jigsaw or band-saw, but cutting by hand with a coping saw will be slow. You could, of course, do your own design for these, which does not involve curves. The angled cut on the stand base where it joins the back piece is more difficult to do by hand. A good way to tackle it is to make a deep mitre box with a slot at the required angle to ensure a constant angle as you cut down the width of the pieces.

Tools and materials

- Pencil
- Flexible rule
- Saw
- Band-saw, jigsaw or coping saw
- Drill
- Screwdriver
- Set square
- Clamps
- 6 doz 3.8 cm (1½ in) No. 8 screws
- 300 ml pack waterproof glue
- 3 doz tacks
- Wood preservative

Timber cutting list

Part	Quantity	Dimensions (L × W × Th)
Long back piece	1 (Planed timber)	134.6 × 15.2 × 1.9 cm 53 × 6 × ¾ in
Middle back pieces	2 (Planed timber)	83.8 × 15.2 × 1.9 cm 33 × 6 × ¾ in
Short back pieces	2 (Planed timber)	33 × 15.2 × 1.9 cm 13 × 6 × ¾ in
Bases with mitred ends	13 (Planed timber)	15.2 × 15.2 × 1.9 cm 6 × 6 × ¾ in
Retainers, shaped	13 (Planed timber)	7.6 × 15.2 × 1.9 cm 3 × 6 × ¾ in

Back pieces

1 First mark out the curved ends on all your back and retainer pieces. You can then cut them out using a band-saw, an electric jigsaw, or by hand with a coping saw.

2 Drill holes in the back pieces top and bottom for the fixing screws.

3 At each level where you want a platform, drill two holes for the screws. These come through the back piece from the back into the stand base. Because of the angle you need to make sure the screws go into the bases at the bottom of the angled edge, to ensure that the screws don't break through the surface of the base. Use a set square to get the holes level.

Base pieces

1 Decide on the angle of forward lean you want, and cut the base pieces out. Note that one end of the base piece is square, while the other end which fits on to the back piece, has the angle.

2 Screw up and glue the end retainers on to the square end of the bases. Be careful to check that it is the right way up, otherwise you'll find your retainer pointing downwards when you come to mount the base on to the back.

3 Mounting the bases on to the back is made easier by a simple trick. Clamp a set square on to the back with its edge above the screw holes. You can then offer up the base to the assembly knowing it will be square across the back piece. Also by adjusting the height of the square above the holes, you can ensure that the screws don't break through the surface of the base.

Finishing

When you have finished you will need to treat the structures with an appropriate preservative. These come in many colours and can be both spirit- and water-based. The water-based ones are usually the most environmentally friendly.

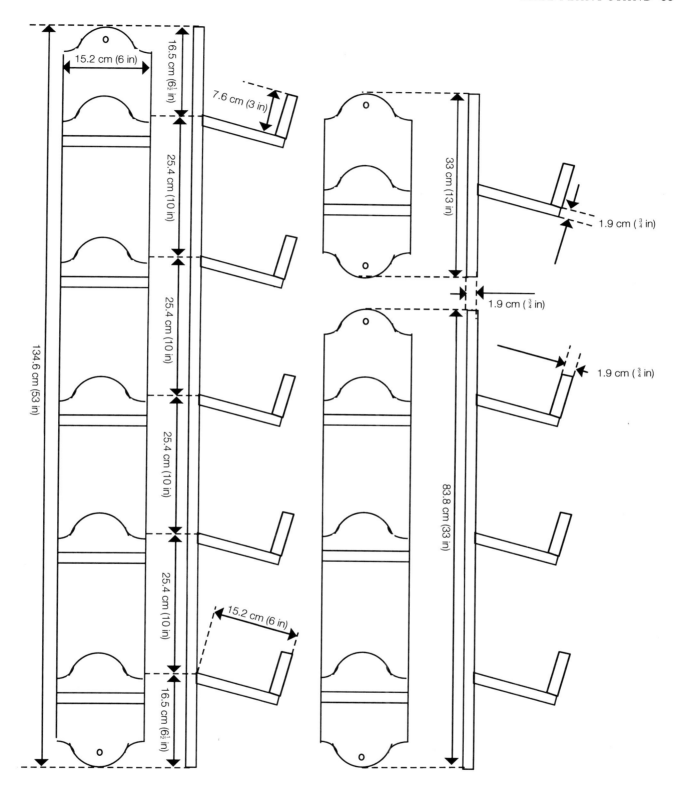

FIGURE 4.1 Wall plant stand: cutting patterns

Dovecot

A dovecot makes an unusual feature in a corner of the garden. Many that you see are purely ornamental but this one is also a working dovecot, so if you are thinking of keeping doves this will make the ideal home for them.

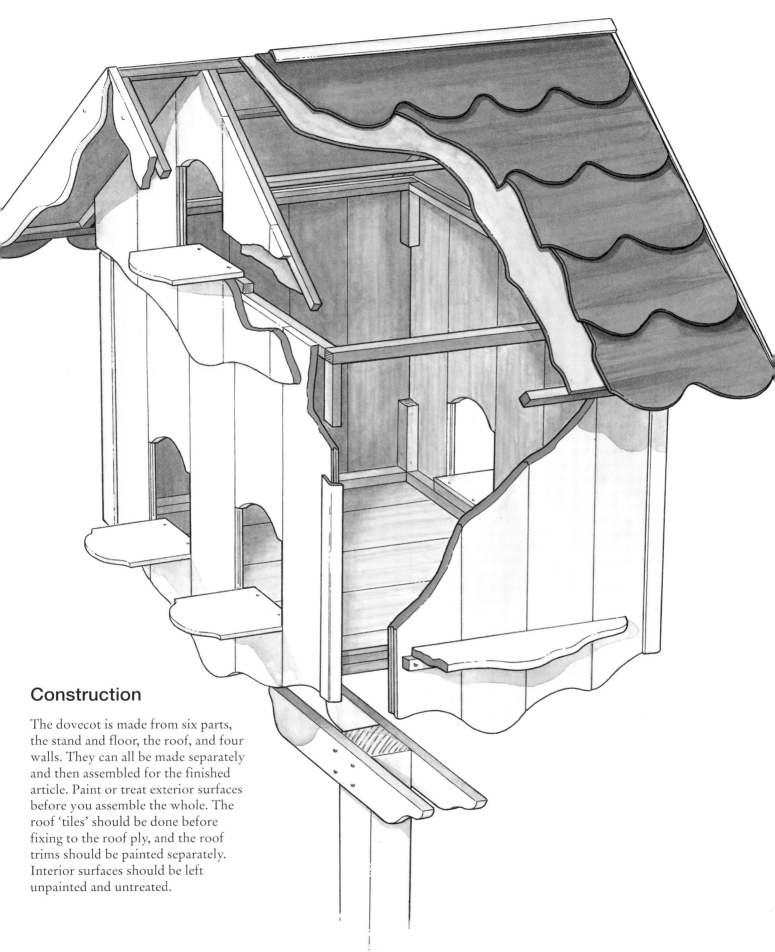

Construction

The dovecot is made from six parts, the stand and floor, the roof, and four walls. They can all be made separately and then assembled for the finished article. Paint or treat exterior surfaces before you assemble the whole. The roof 'tiles' should be done before fixing to the roof ply, and the roof trims should be painted separately. Interior surfaces should be left unpainted and untreated.

Tools and materials

- Pencil
- Flexible rule
- Saw
- Drill
- Screwdriver
- Jigsaw or coping saw
- Hammer
- Set square
- 6 doz 3.8 cm (1½ in) No.8 screws
- 300 ml pack waterproof glue
- 3 doz tacks
- Paint or wood preservative

Timber cutting list

Part	Quantity	Dimensions (L × W × Th)
Hole-wall upper and lower battens	4 (Battening)	56.5 × 2.5 × 1.9 cm 22¼ × 1 × ¾ in
Blank-wall upper and lower battens	4 (Battening)	51.5 × 2.5 × 1.9 cm 20¼ × 1 × ¾ in
Blank-wall side trim supports	2 (Battening)	51.5 × 2.5 × 1.9 cm 20¼ × 1 × ¾ in
Wall joining blocks	8 (Battening)	10.2 × 2.5 × 1.9 cm 4 × 1 × ¾ in
Hole-wall top blocks	2 (Battening)	15.2 × 2.5 × 1.9 cm 6 × 1 × ¾ in
Roof ply long battens	3 (Battening)	83.8 × 2.5 × 1.9 cm 33 × 1 × ¾ in
Roof ply short battens	8 (Battening)	53.3 × 2.5 × 1.9 cm 21 × 1 × ¾ in
Roof ply cross battens	2 (Battening)	52.5 × 2.5 × 1.9 cm 20¾ × 1 × ¾ in
Internal shelf supports	4 (Battening)	11.5 × 2.5 × 1.9 cm 4½ × 1 × ¾ in
Shelf roosting-bar support blocks	4 (Battening)	3.8 × 2.5 × 1.9 cm 1½ × 1 × ¾ in
Roosting bars	5 (Battening)	56.5 × 2.5 × 1.9 cm 22¼ × 1 × ¾ in
Roof pieces	2 (4 mm ($\frac{5}{32}$ in) ply)	83.8 × 57.2 cm 33 × 22½ in
Roof 'tiles'	10 (4 mm ($\frac{5}{32}$ in) ply)	83.8 × 20.3 cm 33 × 8 in
Triangular gable ends	2 (4 mm ($\frac{5}{32}$ in) ply)	66 × 46.7 × 46.7 26 × 18⅜ × 18⅜ in
Wall corner trim	4 (Moulding)	49.5 cm 19½ in
Roof top trim	1 (Moulding)	86.4 cm 34 in
Floor	5 (Tongue & groove floorboard)	56.5 × 11.3 × 2.2 cm 22¼ × 4$\frac{7}{16}$ × ⅞ in
Floor support struts	2 (T & G floorboard)	56.5 × 11.3 × 2.2 cm 22¼ × 4$\frac{7}{16}$ × ⅞ in
Internal shelves	5 (T & G floorboard)	56.5 × 11.3 × 2.2 cm 22¼ × 4$\frac{7}{16}$ × ⅞ in
Walls	20 (T & G 'V' board)	61 × 11.3 × 1.3 cm 24 × 4$\frac{7}{16}$ × ½ in
Blank wall side trims	2 (T & G 'V' board)	56.5 × 11.3 × 1.3 cm 22¼ × 4$\frac{7}{16}$ × ½ in

Gable end trims	4 (T & G 'V' board)	$59 \times 11.3 \times 1.3$ cm $23\frac{1}{4} \times 4\frac{7}{16} \times \frac{1}{2}$ in
Gable end cladding (middle)	2 (T & G 'V' board)	$45.7 \times 11.3 \times 1.3$ cm $18 \times 4\frac{7}{16} \times \frac{1}{2}$ in
Gable end cladding (inner)	4 (T & G 'V' board)	$38.1 \times 11.3 \times 1.3$ cm $15 \times 4\frac{7}{16} \times \frac{1}{2}$ in
Gable end cladding (outer)	4 (T & G 'V' board)	$25.4 \times 11.3 \times 1.3$ cm $10 \times 4\frac{7}{16} \times \frac{1}{2}$ in

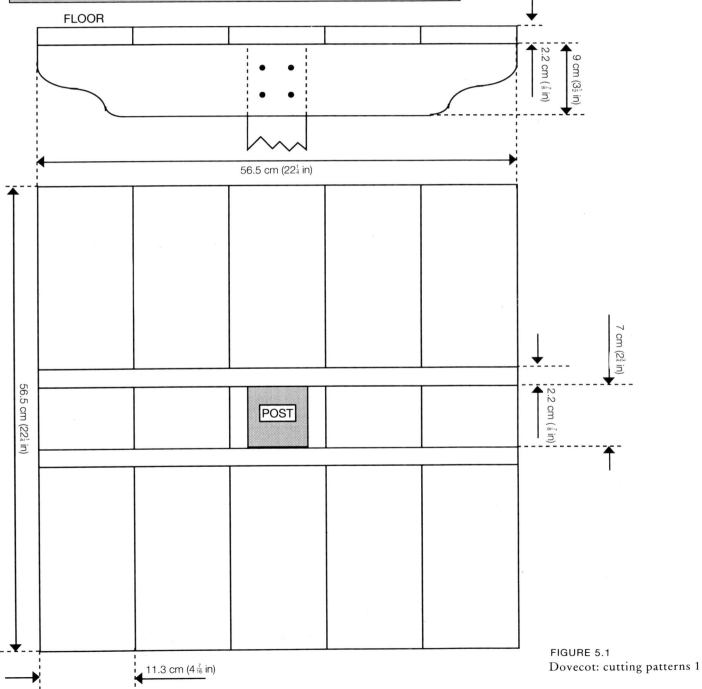

FIGURE 5.1
Dovecot: cutting patterns 1

Floor

1 First make the floor of the dovecot (see figure 5.1). Cut the tongue and groove (T & G) floorboard to length and assemble as a square.

2 Cut the two support struts out of the T & G floorboard, plane off the tongue and the groove, and shape the ends.

3 Lay the post you are going to use between the two support struts, and clamp them together. This keeps the support struts the correct distance apart, while you fix the floorboards to them with screws through the floorboards into the support struts.

Walls

1 Cut the 'V' groove T & G board to length (see figures 5.2 and 5.3), and assemble all four walls.

2 Cut the upper and lower battens and fix in position by screwing through the battens into the walls. Note that the walls with pigeon holes have full-width battens, and the blank walls have 2.5 cm (1 in) clear at each end, to allow the walls to fit together on final assembly.

3 Draw a line on the second and fourth board in each hole wall using the lower batten as a rule. Remove the screws from them and slide the boards out.

4 Draw in the upper profile of the hole as shown in the plan, and then cut the boards. The bits you have cut out then go to make the landing platforms.

5 Slide the top piece of each board back into place and then refix with the screws.

6 Then slide the bottom piece in until it is flush with the top of the lower batten and fix.

7 Mark out the pattern on the lower end of all the walls and cut to shape. You can use either a coping saw or an electric jigsaw if you have one.

8 The side trims for the blank walls are made from a length of 'V' board. Cut two pieces to length and plane off the tongue and the groove.

9 Mark up the same pattern as for the bottom of the walls, along the length of these two boards and cut them out.

10 Cut the support batten to length and shape the ends.

11 Fix these in position on the walls, screwing through into the walls, and then fix the side trims to them by screwing down into the fixing battens.

12 Fix the short jointing battens to the hole walls. Then fix a short batten to the centre of the top of each hole wall, with its edge flush with the wall.

Assembling the carcase

1 Position the four walls with their lower battens on the dovecot floor. The hole walls should be opposite each other. Fix the walls together by screwing through the joining battens into the blank walls.

2 Fix screws through the lower battens into the floor.

3 Fix the platforms through the holes by screwing the inner flat end flush with the inner edge of the lower batten.

4 Cut four roosting bars and shape the rounded edges. Position two about 20.3 cm (8 in) apart across from the lower batten of one blank wall to the other. Screw them down into the lower battens.

5 Cut the two shelves and their support battens to length.

6 Fix the support battens on the hole walls about 25.4 cm (10 in) up from the floor. They should be parallel to the floor and have one end butted up against the blank wall.

7 Position the shelves on the supports and screw into position.

8 Fix support battens for two roosting bars positioned so they form a raised lip to the shelf. Leave a gap between bar and shelf to facilitate cleaning. The shelf and lip together will then be about 15.2 cm (6 in) in width.

9 Cut and shape another roosting bar and fix across the tops of the centre of the hole wall. You will find this one needs to be a bit shorter than the others. It screws into place on the upper batten just inside the two short battens on the wall tops.

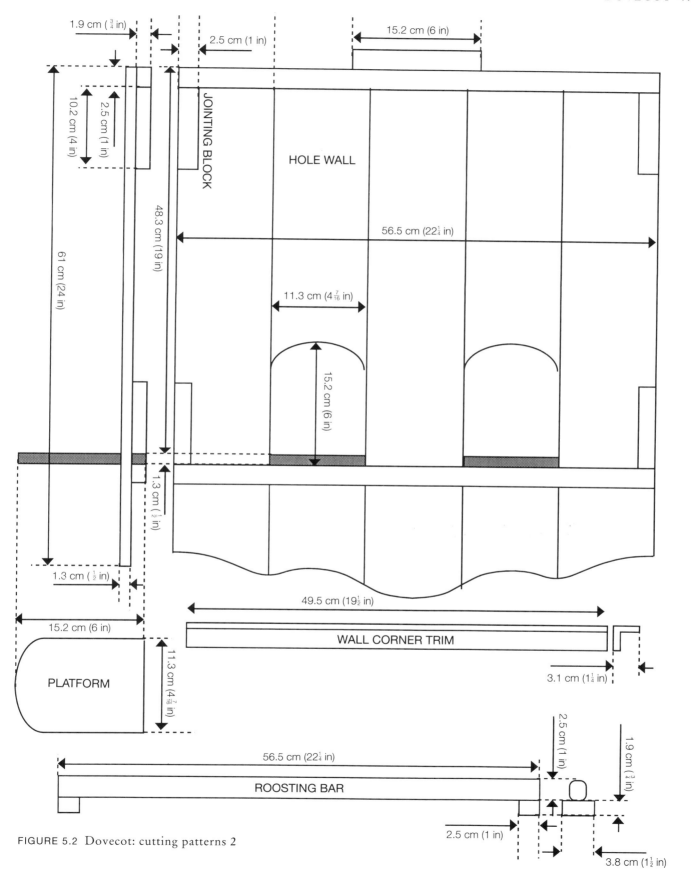

FIGURE 5.2 Dovecot: cutting patterns 2

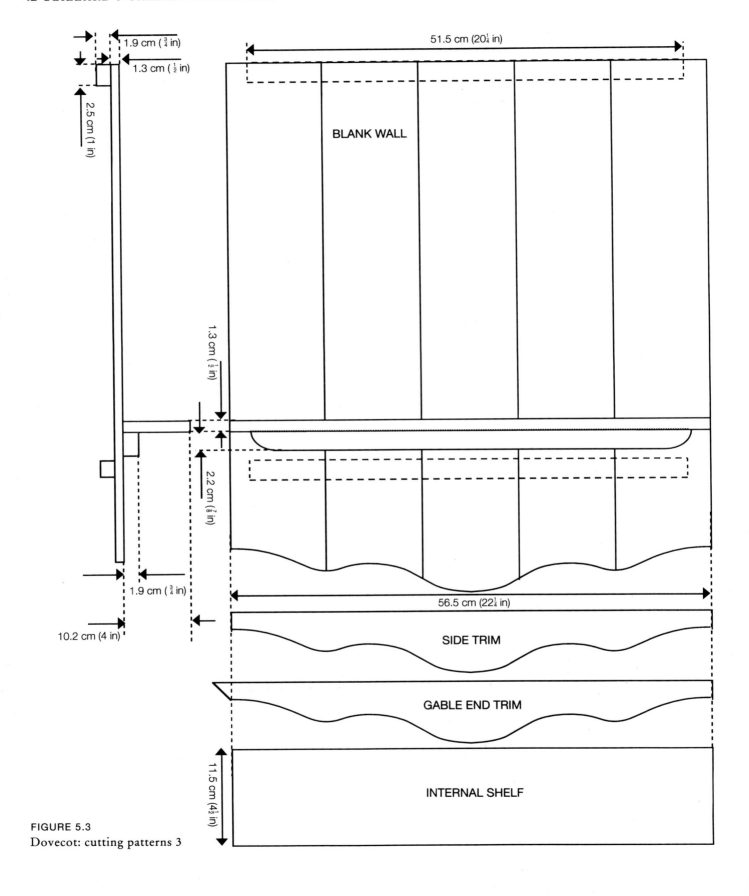

1.9 cm ($\frac{3}{4}$ in)

1.3 cm ($\frac{1}{2}$ in)

2.5 cm (1 in)

51.5 cm (20$\frac{1}{4}$ in)

BLANK WALL

1.3 cm ($\frac{1}{2}$ in)

2.2 cm ($\frac{7}{8}$ in)

1.9 cm ($\frac{3}{4}$ in)

56.5 cm (22$\frac{1}{4}$ in)

10.2 cm (4 in)

SIDE TRIM

GABLE END TRIM

11.5 cm (4$\frac{1}{2}$ in)

INTERNAL SHELF

FIGURE 5.3
Dovecot: cutting patterns 3

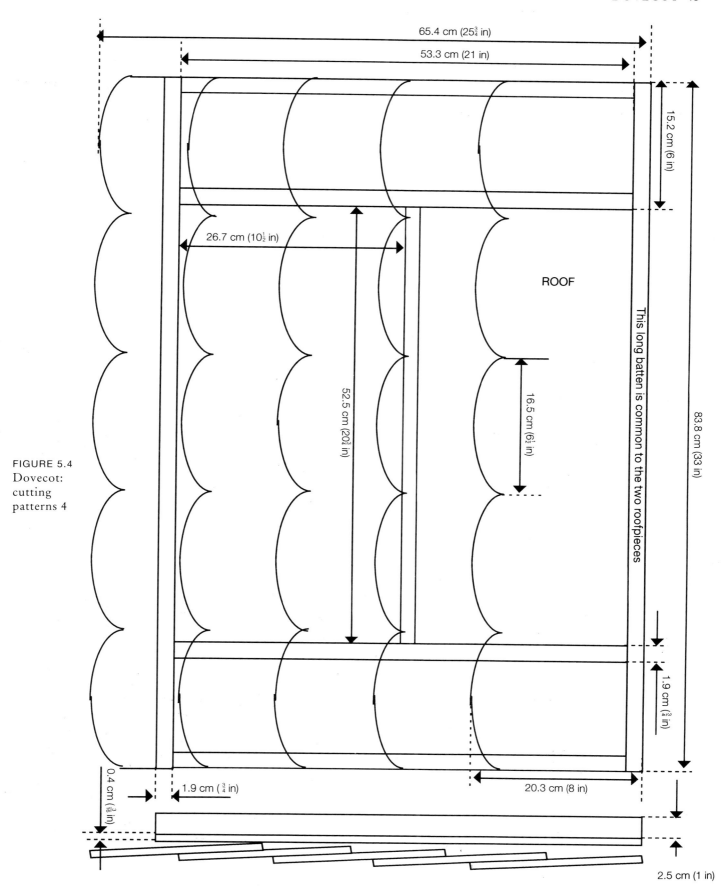

65.4 cm (25¾ in)

53.3 cm (21 in)

15.2 cm (6 in)

26.7 cm (10½ in)

ROOF

52.5 cm (20¾ in)

83.8 cm (33 in)

16.5 cm (6¼ in)

This long batten is common to the two roofpieces

FIGURE 5.4
Dovecot:
cutting
patterns 4

1.9 cm (¾ in)

0.4 cm (³⁄₁₆ in)

1.9 cm (¾ in)

20.3 cm (8 in)

2.5 cm (1 in)

Roof

1 Cut the two pieces of roof ply to size. (See figure 5.4.) Cut the three long battens, the eight short battens, and the two cross battens to length.

2 Fix the battening on to the ply. One roof ply has two long lengths on, and the other only has one, because one is common to the two halves of the roof.

3 Cut out the two gable end pieces of ply. These are equilateral right-angle triangles with a 2.5 cm (1 in) notch taken out of the right-angle corner, and a rectangular piece taken

out of the middle of the long side to allow another pigeon hole.

4 Cut the 'V' board cladding to length (one 45.7 cm (18 in), two 38.1 cm (15 in) and two 25.4 cm (10 in) per gable. (See figure 5.5.)

5 Assemble on the ply so that the inner top corner of each piece is flush with the edge of the ply, and they are flush along the bottom.

6 Screw the ply on making sure the 'V' shows on the outside.

7 Trim the corners off above the ply.

8 The centre board on each gable is then marked up for the hole. The flat bottom mark is 2.5 cm (1 in) above the long edge of the ply. Unscrew and remove these two centre boards from the gables.

9 Mark up the top profile of the hole and cut it out. Keep the cut-out for the platform.

GABLE END

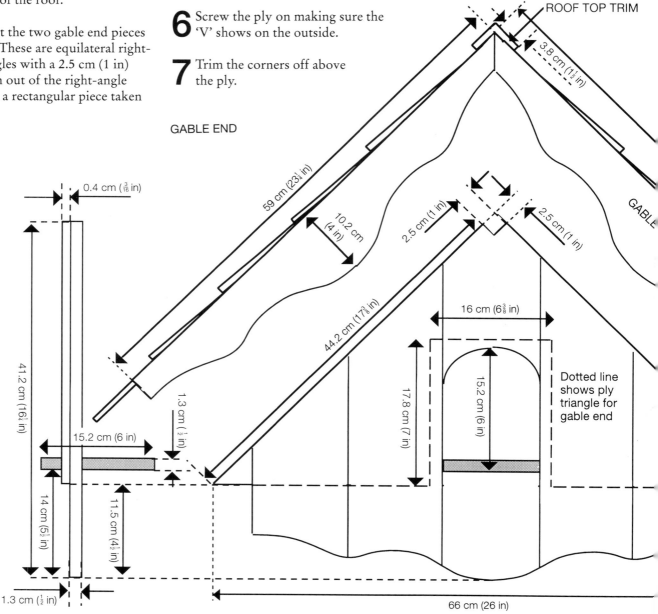

10 Refix the rest. The top screws back in as was, but you will need to glue the bottom half along its tongues and grooves, because there is no ply under it to fix to.

11 Trace out and then cut out the bottom pattern.

12 Position the two gable ends on the outer surface of the short batten at each end of the roof piece with the two long battens. Fix them by screwing through the gable into the batten. Then fix the other roof piece in the same. Also screw the top edge to the top (now shared) long batten.

13 Offer up the roof to the carcase to make sure it fits exactly. The bottom edges of the gable ply should rest on the hole-wall top with the two short-wall top battens fitting in the holes in the ply. The top surface of these battens should be flush with the bottom of the gable pigeon-hole. The inner surface of the gable cladding should overlap the outer surface of the wall tops. If you have to adjust it, you can do so by unscrewing the battens to which one gable end is attached, from the roof ply, and refixing in the corrected position.

14 Mark up and cut the ten roof 'tiles'. The tiles should be painted or treated before fixing to the roof ply, and the roof trims should be painted separately.

15 Fix the roof tiles, starting with the lower one on each side and overlapping them so they are spread evenly up the roof. Screw right through the ply into the battens underneath.

16 Cut out and mark the pattern on the four gable-end trims. Note that they are the same as the wall side trims except that the inner ends are slightly extended and mitred at 45 degrees so that they all fit together neatly.

17 The job is finished off by cutting and applying the mouldings to the corners of the walls and the roof top.

18 When you screw the gable-hole platforms down on to the battens on top of the walls, you will find this fixes the roof down on to the carcase so leave this until last. To remove the roof for cleaning later, you will have to unscrew these platforms. Interior surfaces should be left unpainted and untreated.

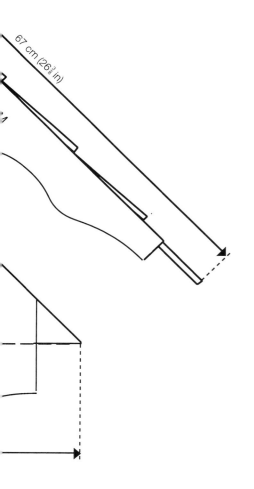

67 cm (26⅜ in)

FIGURE 5.5 Dovecot: cutting patterns 5

Oriental Bird Table

There can be fewer greater pleasures than watching garden birds feeding. Your bird table should be left in place all year round, because there are even times in the summer when there is not much food for small birds. Autumn, when the nuts and berries are out, is the easiest time for birds. Once your bird table is in place you should make sure that you are feeding the birds the correct foods for the time of year. You can get all the information you need in this respect from the Royal Society for the Protection of Birds.

Construction

The table is best placed on a post at shoulder height, and in a clear space. The roof keeps off some of the snow in winter, and you can easily hang nut baskets from the timbers. If you get the roof levels right you can stop some of the bigger birds like rooks getting at the food on the table.

Tables and materials

- Pencil
- Flexible rule
- Saw
- Plane
- Clamps
- String
- Drill
- Countersink bit
- Screwdriver
- Jigsaw or coping saw
- Hammer
- Set square
- 2 doz 3.8 cm (1½ in) No. 8 screws
- 300 ml pack waterproof glue
- 4 small brackets
- 4 small hinges (3.8 – 5.1 cm (1½ – 2 in) in length)
- Paint or wood preservative

Timber cutting list

Part	Quantity	Dimensions (L × W × Th)
Post	1 (Timber)	1.8 m × 7.6 × 7.6 cm 6 ft × 3 × 3 in
Table supports	2 (Timbers)	30.5 × 5.1 × 2.5 cm 12 × 2 × 1 in
Table	2 (Planking)	45.7 × 22.9 × 2.5 cm 18 × 9 × 1 in
Vertical roof supports	4 (Timbers)	17.8 × 5.1 × 2.5 cm 7 × 2 × 1 in
Decorative horizontal roof timbers	4 (Timbers)	27.9 × 12.7 × 2.5 cm 11 × 5 × 1 in
Roof pieces	4 (3 mm (⅛ in) exterior ply)	91.4 × 91.4 cm × 3 mm 36 × 36 × ⅛ in
Square roof capping piece	1 (3 mm (⅛ in) exterior ply)	12.7 × 12.7 cm × 3 mm 5 × 5 × ⅛ in
Tapered dowel	1 (Dowelling)	10.2 × 1.3 cm 4 × ½ in

Post

1 The starting point for the construction of the Oriental bird table is the 1.8 m (6 ft) length of 7.6 × 7.6 cm (3 × 3 in) timber. Check that the ends are cut squarely, and then use a plane to bevel the four corners at the top. (See figure 6.1.) The bevels should end up about 30.5 cm (12 in) long and 2.5 cm (1 in) wide along its length. The post is now ready to have the rest of the structure added to it, so you should put it to one side while you prepare the other bits.

Table

1 The table itself is made from two 45.7 cm (18 in) pieces of 22.9 × 2.5 cm (9 × 1 in) timber. (See figure 6.2.) Clamp them together on the bench, and use a piece of string pivoted in the middle to scribe a 22.9 cm (9 in) circle on the wood. It just fits!

2 Separate the two pieces and cut around the lines with a jigsaw to give two semicircles.

3 Next cut the hole in the middle of the circle through which the post will fit. This is achieved by cutting a hole 7.6 cm (3 in) long and 3.8 cm (1½ in) deep around the middle of the straight side of each semicircle. When you put them together they should have a 7.6 cm (3 in) square hole in the middle of the circular piece formed by the semicircles.

4 Cut the two table support struts, and screw and glue them into position 33 cm (13 in) from the top of the post.

5 Place the two table pieces around the post resting on top of the supports and screw and glue them into position.

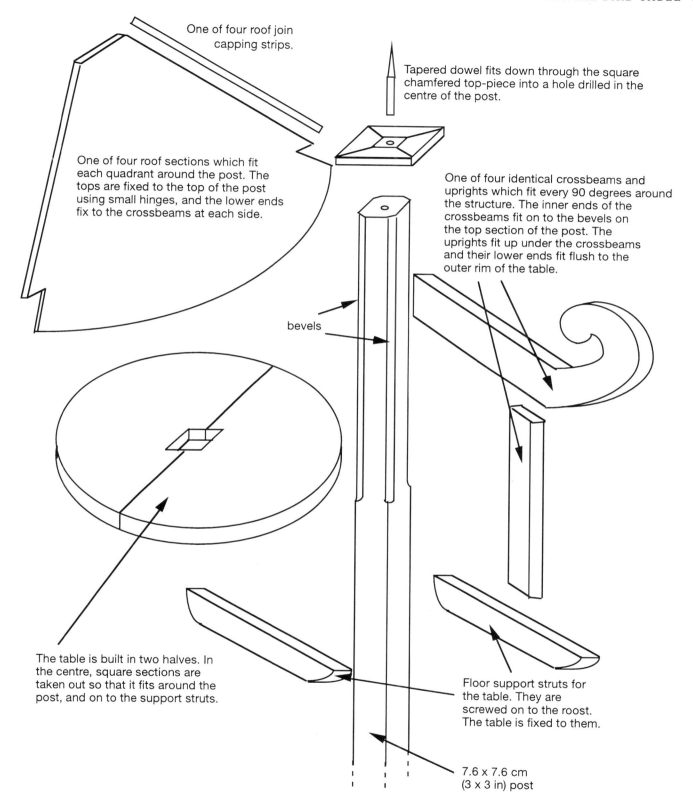

One of four roof join capping strips.

Tapered dowel fits down through the square chamfered top-piece into a hole drilled in the centre of the post.

One of four roof sections which fit each quadrant around the post. The tops are fixed to the top of the post using small hinges, and the lower ends fix to the crossbeams at each side.

One of four identical crossbeams and uprights which fit every 90 degrees around the structure. The inner ends of the crossbeams fit on to the bevels on the top section of the post. The uprights fit up under the crossbeams and their lower ends fit flush to the outer rim of the table.

bevels

The table is built in two halves. In the centre, square sections are taken out so that it fits around the post, and on to the support struts.

Floor support struts for the table. They are screwed on to the roost. The table is fixed to them.

7.6 x 7.6 cm (3 x 3 in) post

FIGURE 6.1 Oriental bird table

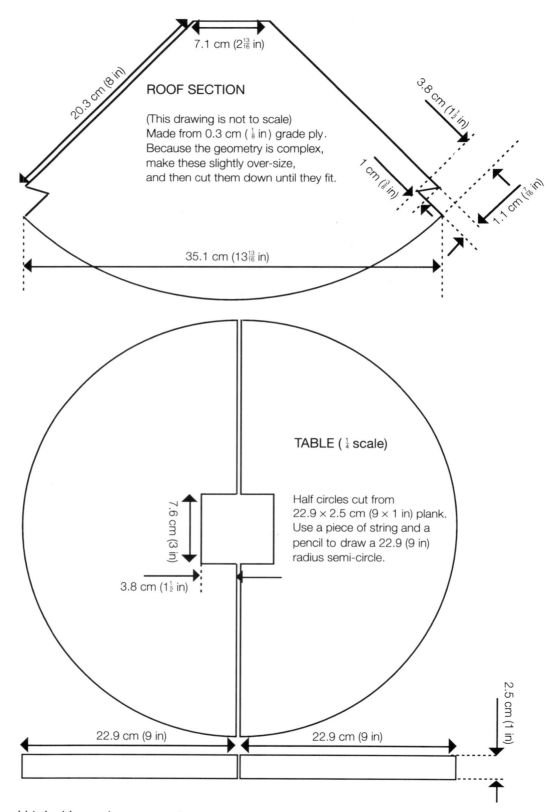

7.1 cm ($2\frac{13}{16}$ in)

20.3 cm (8 in)

3.8 cm ($1\frac{1}{2}$ in)

ROOF SECTION

(This drawing is not to scale)
Made from 0.3 cm ($\frac{1}{8}$ in) grade ply.
Because the geometry is complex,
make these slightly over-size,
and then cut them down until they fit.

1 cm ($\frac{3}{8}$ in)

1.1 cm ($\frac{7}{16}$ in)

35.1 cm ($13\frac{13}{16}$ in)

TABLE ($\frac{1}{4}$ scale)

7.6 cm (3 in)

Half circles cut from
22.9 × 2.5 cm (9 × 1 in) plank.
Use a piece of string and a
pencil to draw a 22.9 (9 in)
radius semi-circle.

3.8 cm ($1\frac{1}{2}$ in)

2.5 cm (1 in)

22.9 cm (9 in)

22.9 cm (9 in)

FIGURE 6.2 Oriental bird table: cutting patterns 1

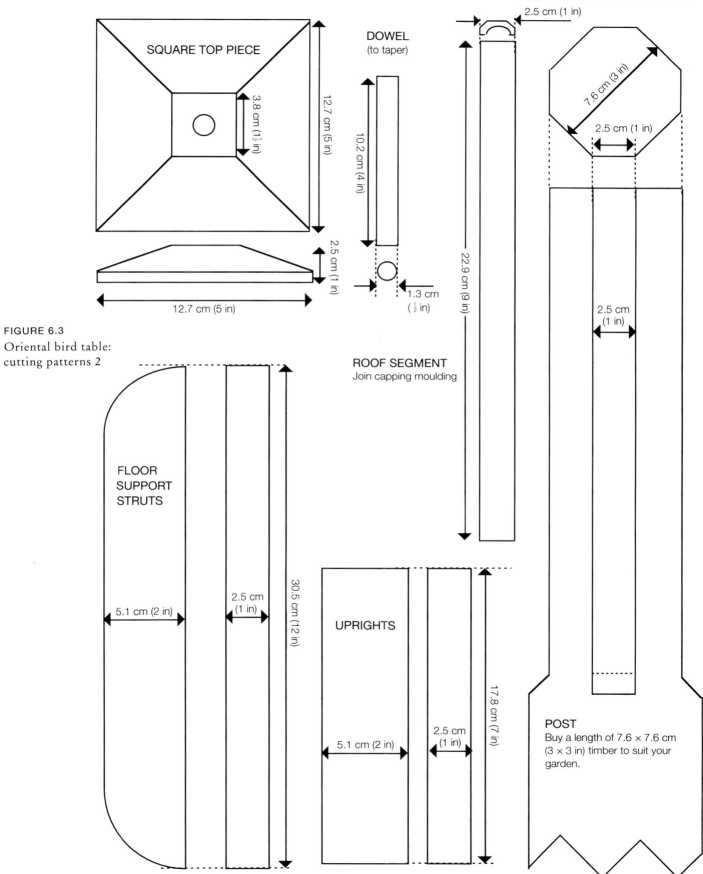

SQUARE TOP PIECE

12.7 cm (5 in)

3.8 cm (1½ in)

2.5 cm (1 in)

12.7 cm (5 in)

DOWEL
(to taper)

10.2 cm (4 in)

1.3 cm (½ in)

2.5 cm (1 in)

7.6 cm (3 in)

2.5 cm (1 in)

2.5 cm (1 in)

22.9 cm (9 in)

ROOF SEGMENT
Join capping moulding

FIGURE 6.3
Oriental bird table:
cutting patterns 2

FLOOR
SUPPORT
STRUTS

5.1 cm (2 in)

2.5 cm (1 in)

30.5 cm (12 in)

UPRIGHTS

5.1 cm (2 in)

2.5 cm (1 in)

17.8 cm (7 in)

POST
Buy a length of 7.6 × 7.6 cm
(3 × 3 in) timber to suit your
garden.

Roof

1 Next cut the four lengths for the vertical roof supports of the bird table. (See figure 6.3.)

2 Draw out the shape of the decorative horizontals on to 2.5 cm (1 in) timber. (See figure 6.4.) It is the curling shape of these that gives the bird table some of its oriental flavour, so take some care to get the shape right.

3 Put one of the vertical support pieces on the table flush with the outside rim and opposite one of the bevels on the post. Place the horizontal decorative piece on top of the vertical with its base against the bevel. Mark up where the two join.

4 Remove and screw and glue the two pieces together.

5 Repeat the process for the other three bevels.

6 These pieces are then fixed to the table by screwing and glueing up through the bottom of the table into the vertical leg, and by using a small right-angled bracket to join the horizontal and the post.

7 To make the roof first measure the triangles between each of the four support pieces and mark out and cut them from 3 mm ($\frac{1}{8}$ in) exterior grade ply.

8 Use small hinges to attach each roof panel to the post at the appropriate point. Cut out the small notches in the panels that allow them to sit neatly and securely on the horizontals.

9 Glue the decorative strips of mouldings over the joins between the roof panels.

FIGURE 6.4 Template

Full scale template

Mark up and cut four from 2.5 cm (1 in) timber.

10 The capping piece that sits over the top of the roof panels gives the table its two storey pagoda-like appearance. Make it from a square piece of 2.5 cm (1 in). First draw a 3.8 cm (1½ in) square in the centre of the piece and plane the slopes on the little 'roof' leaving the marked square in the middle and about 1.3 cm (½ in) of thickness at the edges. This piece is then glued on to the top of the post.

11 To finish off the top and give it an 'eastern' touch, drill down through the centre of the top for a tapered length of dowel, effectively giving a spike on the top. Glue this into place.

Finish and fixing

1 Finish off your bird table with the blackest and reddest water-based stain preservatives you can find if you want to bring out an extra oriental flavour!

2 There are a variety of ways of fixing your post into the ground. You can use one of the metal ground fixings that are carried in most garden centres, or you can dig out and concrete the post in position. You can even use another post to make a hole and then place the bird table in it. Although this will not be as secure as the other ways, it will allow you to reposition the table more easily.

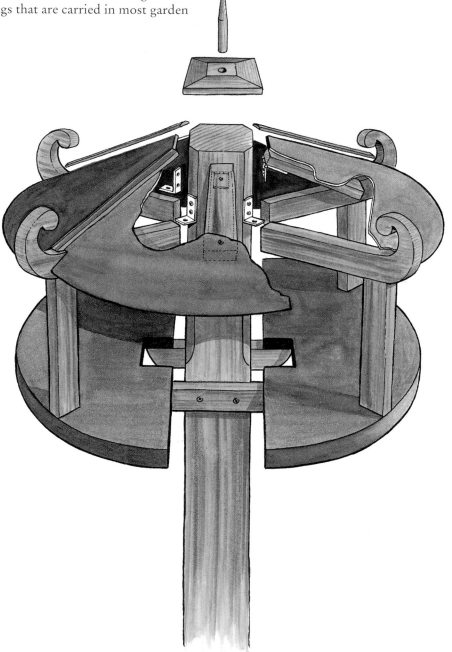

Wildlife Boxes

Urban and rural gardens provide some of the best environments for many birds and small mammals and encouraging them to live in your garden can be rewarding for them and for you.

Barn owls, which are becoming rarer all the time, can be encouraged to nest in your garden if you place a barn owl box in a barn or shed that has constant open access for the birds, or it can be strapped up in a tree to increase the number of nesting 'buildings' for these fine birds of prey.

Hedgehogs are great at pest control, devouring large quantities of slugs, beetles, caterpillars and earwigs. Encourage this delightful mammal to live in your garden by building a hedgehog box.

Construction

Both boxes are easy to make. You could do the roof and walls of the owl box in ply, but it looks better using shiplap, and will allow more air to circulate between the boards. It is a good idea to fix one side of the roof with screws only so that you can get in to clean the box out if you have to. You never know who's going to take up residence!

The hedgehog box is a very simple project built from Nordic redwood or whitewood. Basically it's a box with a roof and a floor. The front has a 'door' cut in it to which a tunnel is attached to allow the hedgehog to enter.

Timber cutting list (Barn owl box)

Part	Quantity	Dimensions (L × W × Th)
Floor	1 (1.9 cm (¾ in) shuttering ply)	76.2 × 38.1 × 1.9 cm 30 × 15 × ¾ in
Back, front and intermediate walls	3 (6 mm (¼ in) ply)	40.6 × 38.1 × 6 mm 16 × 15 × ¼ in
Triangular gable tops	3 (6 mm (¼ in) ply)	25.4 × 25.4 × 25.4 cm 10 × 10 × 10 in
Cover boards for side walls	8 (Shiplap boards)	51.5 × 11.5 cm 20¼ × 4½ in
Cover boards for roof	6 (Shiplap boards)	53.9 × 11.5 cm 21¼ × 4½ in
Battens for fixing floor and shiplap to ply walls	9.1 m (30 ft) (Battening)	

Tools and materials

- Pencil
- Flexible rule
- Set square
- Saw
- Clamps
- Drill
- Countersink bit
- Screwdriver
- Jigsaw or coping saw
- Glass-paper
- Hammer (Barn owl box)
- 3 doz 2.5 cm (1 in) nails (Barn owl box)
- 5 doz 3 cm (1¼ in) No. 8 screws (Barn owl box)
- 3 doz 3 cm (¼ in) No. 8 screws (Hedgehog box)
- 300 ml pack waterproof glue
- Water-based wood-stain preservative

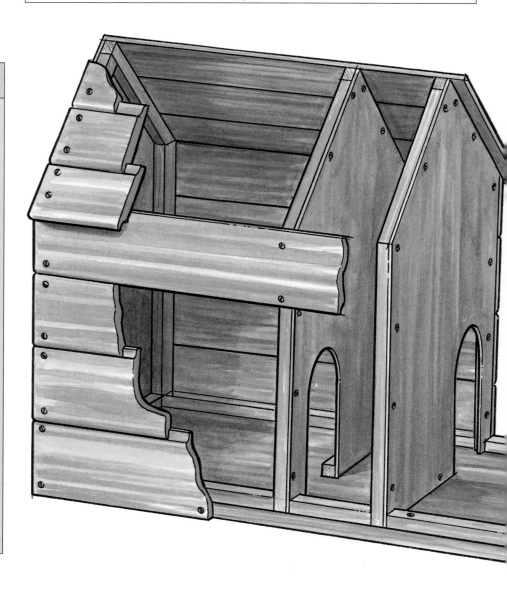

Barn owl box

1 The box is made from the floor upwards (see figures 7.1 and 7.2.). Cut the floor from 1.9 cm ($\frac{3}{4}$ in) shuttering ply or other similarly thick plywood.

2 Measure out the positions of the battens, then screw and glue them into position to provide footing fixings for the walls.

3 Also fix battens around the front 'verandah' to provide edging.

4 Then cut the front, back and intermediate walls from 6 mm ($\frac{1}{4}$ in) ply. (See figure 7.3.) If you can mark one out on a piece of ply and then clamp three sheets together you'll get three identical walls.

5 Cut a door in the front and intermediate walls at the bottom on one side, using a jigsaw to cut the rounded shape for these doors.

6 Before you fit the walls fit battening around the edges except the bottom one.

7 Next screw and glue the walls to the footing battens on the floor. Note that when they are fixed the doors do not line up to give straight line access to the box but are offset on opposite sides forming a chicane.

8 The walls are formed by cladding with shiplap timber, which you screw and glue into the battens on the ply walls.

Finishing

The box should be treated only on the outside, the inside being left bare. The outside can be treated with any good environmentally-friendly preservative, preferably a water-based stain preservative which will not harm the birds. Many of these preserve by water-proofing the wood, and are perfectly safe to handle once they have dried.

Siting the box

The box is best placed in a secluded building away from busy roads or in a tree facing open ground, where it can be seen by a passing owl. Owls are more likely to take up residence if there is a good supply of voles nearby! Tie the box in the hole of the tree. You may have to fix battens to the box which can then be fixed to the tree. Position it so that owlets can walk back into the tray if they fall off. Young owls often fall before they can fly, but they flap and climb back up the trunk of the tree using their claws. If in a building, make sure that the doors can never shut, trapping the birds inside the building. Owls are territorial so don't put boxes close together!

If barn owls take up residence remember they are protected by law and that it is illegal to visit the nest without a licence.

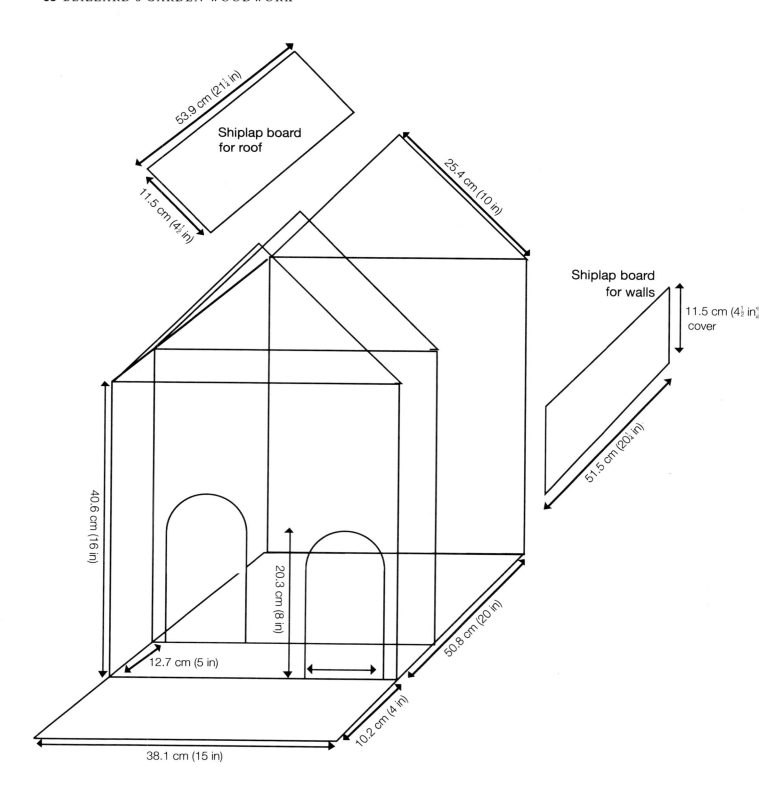

FIGURE 7.1 Owl box: cutting patterns 1

Side elevation without shiplap walls or roof

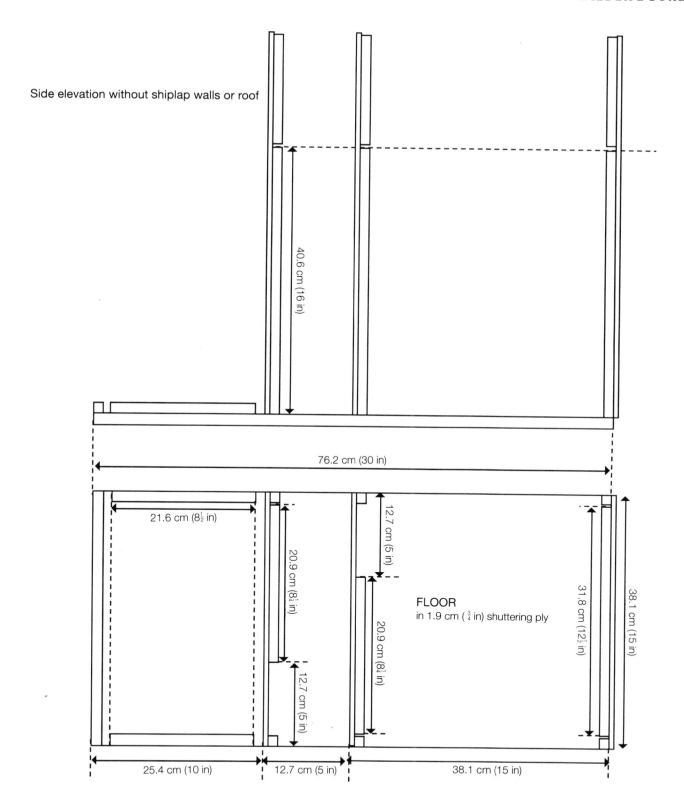

40.6 cm (16 in)

76.2 cm (30 in)

21.6 cm (8½ in)

20.9 cm (8¼ in)

12.7 cm (5 in)

12.7 cm (5 in)

20.9 cm (8¼ in)

FLOOR
in 1.9 cm (¾ in) shuttering ply

31.8 cm (12½ in)

38.1 cm (15 in)

12.7 cm (5 in)

25.4 cm (10 in)

12.7 cm (5 in)

38.1 cm (15 in)

Plan view without shiplap walls or roof

FIGURE 7.2 Owl box: cutting patterns 2

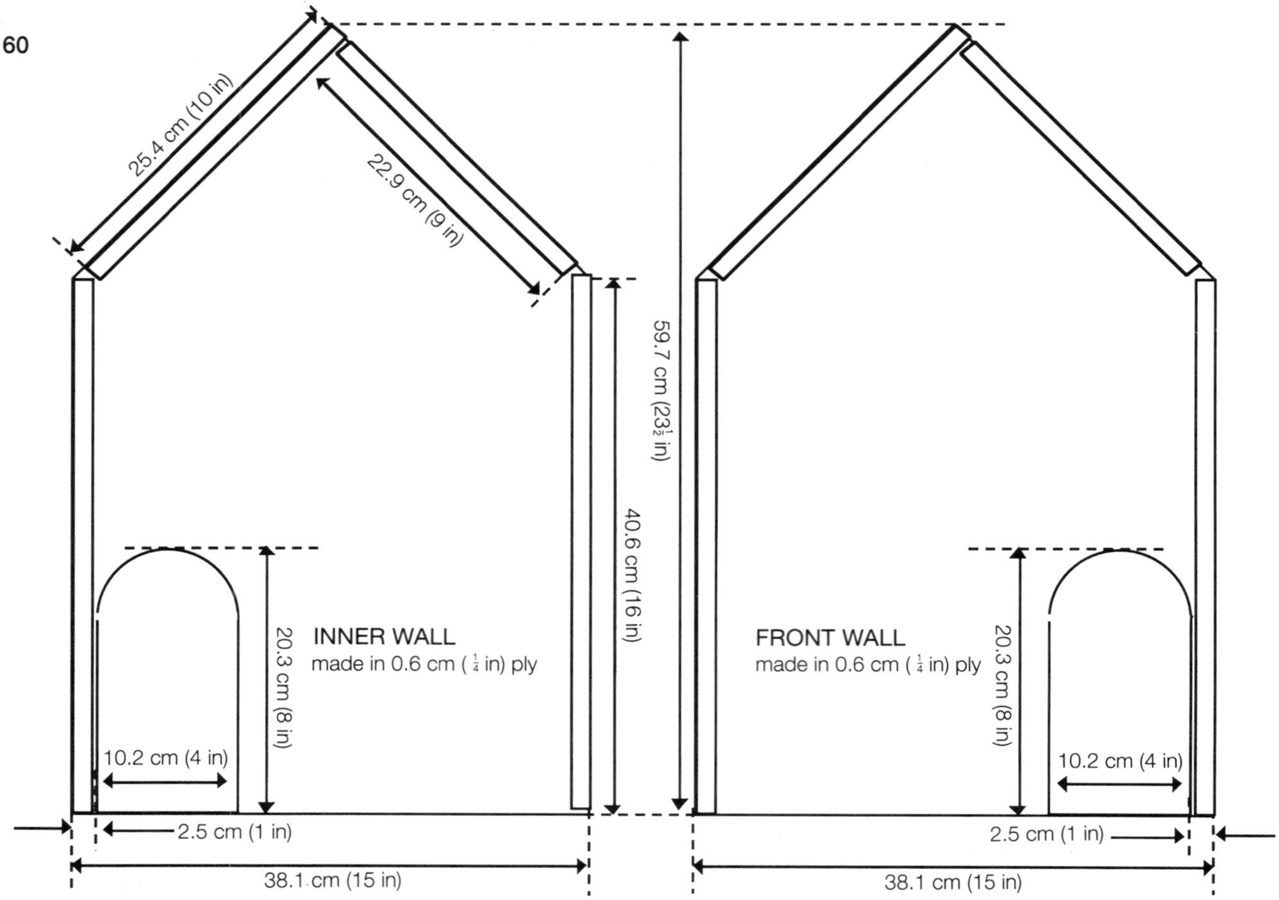

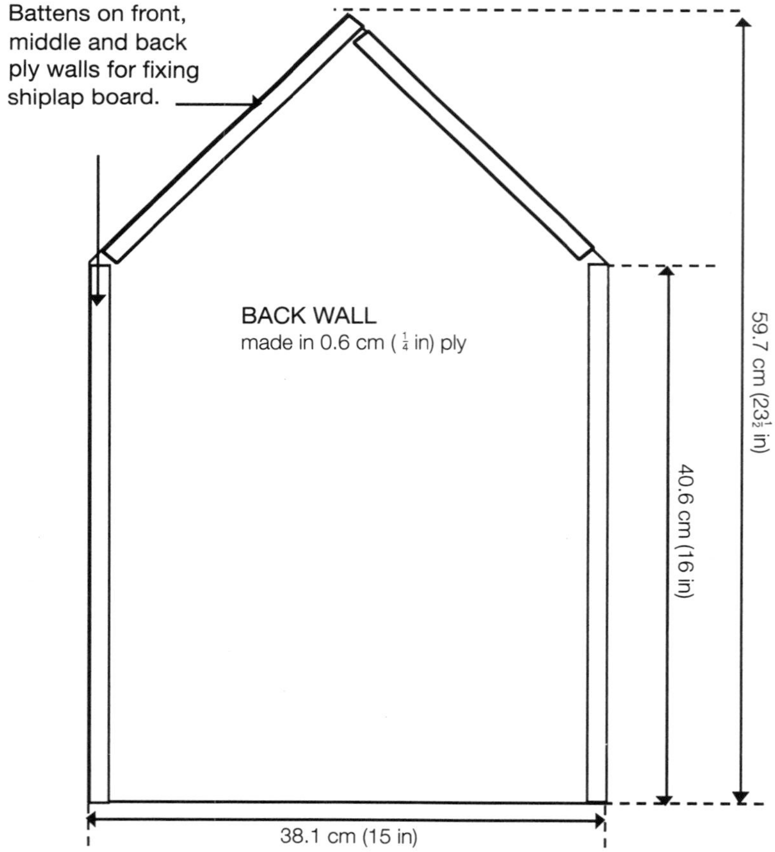

25.4 cm (10 in)

22.9 cm (9 in)

59.7 cm (23½ in)

40.6 cm (16 in)

INNER WALL
made in 0.6 cm (¼ in) ply

20.3 cm (8 in)

10.2 cm (4 in)

2.5 cm (1 in)

38.1 cm (15 in)

FRONT WALL
made in 0.6 cm (¼ in) ply

20.3 cm (8 in)

10.2 cm (4 in)

2.5 cm (1 in)

38.1 cm (15 in)

Battens on front,
middle and back
ply walls for fixing
shiplap board.

BACK WALL
made in 0.6 cm (¼ in) ply

59.7 cm (23½ in)

40.6 cm (16 in)

38.1 cm (15 in)

FIGURE 7.3 Owl box: cutting patterns 3

Timber cutting list (Hedgehog box)

Part	Quantity	Dimensions (L × W × Th)
Box roof	1 (1.9 cm ($\frac{3}{4}$ in) planed timber)	30.5 × 19.1 × 1.9 cm 12 × 7$\frac{1}{2}$ × $\frac{3}{4}$ in
Box floor	1 (1.9 cm ($\frac{3}{4}$ in) planed timber)	30.5 × 19.1 × 1.9 cm 12 × 7$\frac{1}{2}$ × $\frac{3}{4}$ in
Box side walls	2 (1.9 cm ($\frac{3}{4}$ in) planed timber)	22.9 × 19.1 × 1.9 cm 9 × 7$\frac{1}{2}$ × $\frac{3}{4}$ in
Box back	1 (1.9 cm ($\frac{3}{4}$ in) planed timber)	30.5 × 19.1 × 1.9 cm 12 × 7$\frac{1}{2}$ × $\frac{3}{4}$ in
Box front	1 (1.9 cm ($\frac{3}{4}$ in) planed timber)	30.5 × 19.1 × 1.9 cm 12 × 7$\frac{1}{2}$ × $\frac{3}{4}$ in
Box vent	1 (Piece of piping + 90 degree bend)	Approx 12.7 cm × 1.9 cm 5 × $\frac{3}{4}$ in
Tunnel roof	1 (1.9 cm ($\frac{3}{4}$ in) planed timber)	27.3 × 14 × 1.9 cm 10$\frac{3}{4}$ × 5$\frac{1}{2}$ × $\frac{3}{4}$ in
Tunnel side walls	2 (1.9 cm ($\frac{3}{4}$ in) planed timber)	27.3 × 12.1 × 1.9 cm 10$\frac{3}{4}$ × 4$\frac{3}{4}$ × $\frac{3}{4}$ in

Hedgehog box

1 Drill a hole in the box roof large enough to take the piece of plastic tubing (the type used by builders and plumbers for waste pipe). This acts as a breathing vent. To stop rain water going down the tube when the box is placed outside fit a 90 degree bend of the same size tubing on the top.

2 Cut out the walls, floors and roofs. (See figures 7.4 and 7.5.)

3 Cut out the door in the front wall. To do this saw down the vertical sides and then use a coping saw or a jigsaw to cut the other edge.

4 Drill countersink holes for the screws and pilot holes through for the screw to bite into.

5 Screw and glue the side walls on to the floor.

6 Next screw and glue the back wall and roof on.

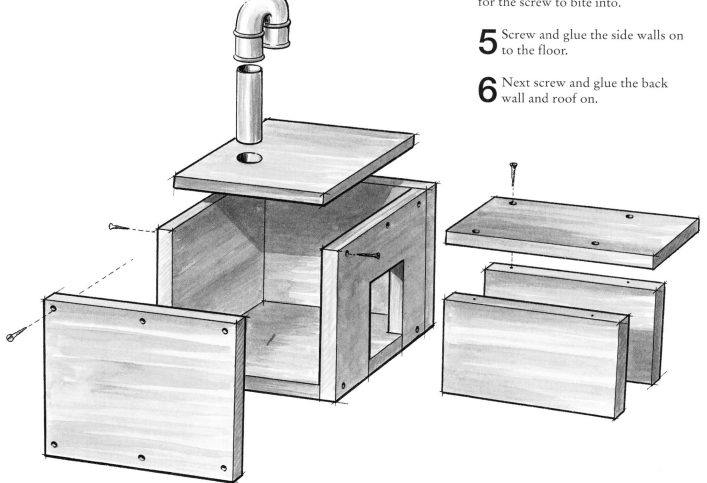

7 Screw and glue the tunnel walls to the tunnel roof.

8 Screw and glue the tunnel around the door in the front wall.

9 Lastly, attach the front wall into the rest of the box.

Finishing

Use a water-based preservative which is safe to use around animals. Don't treat the inside, leave it bare. Water-based preservatives are easy to use and you just wash out your brush under the tap.

Siting the box

Fill the box with dry leaves. Find a sheltered and well-drained part of the garden – a sloping bank is good – or dig the box into the ground underneath some shrubs. Cover the top with a sheet of PVC, and then bury it under at least 25.4 cm (10 in) of soil, leaving the entrance and the breathing pipe clear.

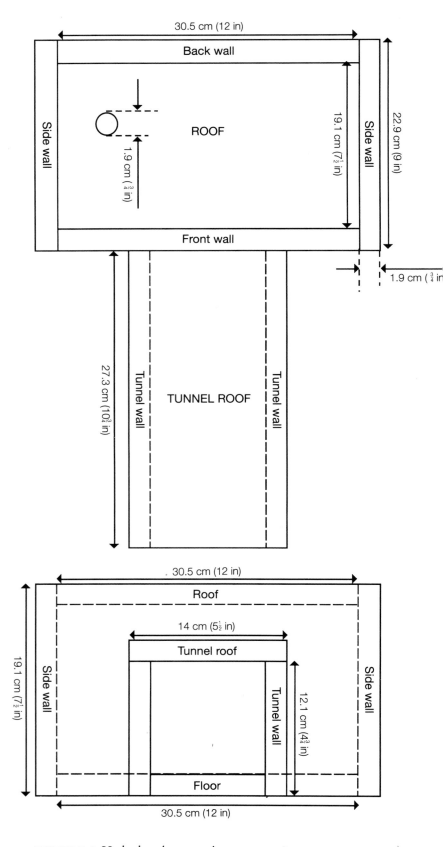

FIGURE 7.4 Hedgehog box: cutting patterns 1

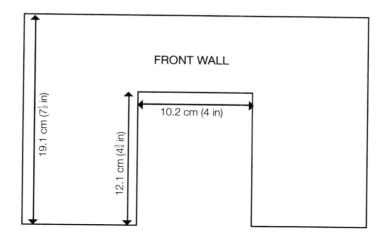

FRONT WALL

19.1 cm (7½ in)

12.1 cm (4¾ in)

10.2 cm (4 in)

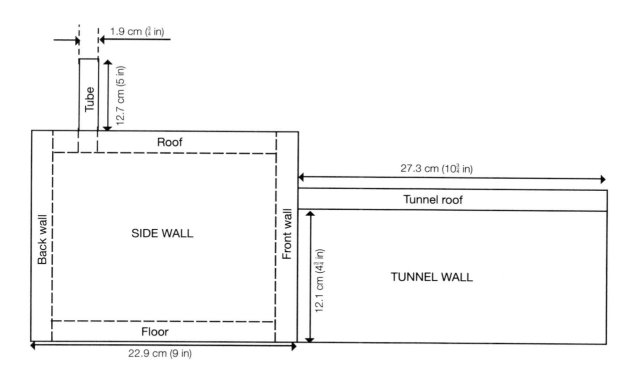

1.9 cm (¾ in)

Tube

12.7 cm (5 in)

Roof

27.3 cm (10¾ in)

Tunnel roof

Back wall

SIDE WALL

Front wall

TUNNEL WALL

12.1 cm (4¾ in)

Floor

22.9 cm (9 in)

Dimensions assume that all the timber is 1.9 cm (¾ in) thick

FIGURE 7.5 Hedgehog box: cutting patterns 2

Colonial Postbox

This is a real fun item. Anyone can have a postbox, but you won't see many like this. It is based on a colonial style house with a verandah, wood plank walls, and shutters on the windows. The upstairs window is the full width and acts as the postbox slit. The roof hinges up so that you can retrieve your post. You can fit a lock on it for security, if you want.

Construction

The colonial postbox is a sturdily built carcase with a plywood roof. The walls and verandah floor are planked with 'mini-planks' to give a New England style. The verandah roof is set into a groove in the front wall of the house and supported on dowel columns at the front. (See figure 8.1.) The construction of the carcase is very simple once you have cut out the carcase components (A to D in the cutting list).

Tools and materials

- Pencil
- Flexible rule
- Set square
- Saw
- Jigsaw or coping saw
- Bench saw, band-saw or coping saw
- Drill
- Countersink bit
- Screwdriver
- Rough plane or router
- Chisel
- Wood mallet
- 5 doz 3 cm (1¼ in) No. 8 screws
- 300 ml pack waterproof glue
- Wood stain preservative

Timber cutting list

Part	Quantity	Dimensions (L × W × Th)
A side wall	2 (Planed timber)	37.4 × 21.6 × 21.6 cm $14\frac{3}{4} \times 8\frac{1}{2} \times 8\frac{1}{2}$ in
B Floor piece	2 (Planed timber)	36.2 × 21.6 cm $14\frac{1}{4} \times 8\frac{1}{2}$ in
C Rear wall	2 (Planed timber)	38.7 × 21.6 cm $15\frac{1}{4} \times 8\frac{1}{2}$ in
D Front wall	1 (Planed timber)	43.6 × 21.6 cm $17\frac{1}{8} \times 8\frac{1}{2}$ in
E Planking	1.8 m (60 ft) (Mini-planking)	1.9 cm × 3 mm $\frac{3}{4} \times \frac{1}{8}$ in
F Ply roof	1 (Ply)	47 × 32.5 cm $18\frac{1}{2} \times 12\frac{3}{4}$ in
G Ply roof tiles	5 (Ply)	47 × 10.2 cm $18\frac{1}{2} \times 4$ in
H Verandah roof	1 (Ply)	43.6 × 10.2 cm $17\frac{1}{8} \times 4$ in
I Rear wall joining piece	1 (Ply)	51 × 9.4 × 1.6 cm $20 \times 3\frac{3}{8} \times \frac{5}{8}$ in
J Dowels	4 (1 cm ($\frac{3}{8}$ in) dowelling)	3.5 × 1 cm $1\frac{3}{16} \times \frac{3}{8}$ in Add 1.3 cm ($\frac{1}{2}$ in) for footing into floor
K Dowels for rails	2 (1 cm ($\frac{3}{8}$ in) dowelling)	14 × 1 cm $5\frac{1}{2} \times \frac{3}{8}$ in
L Dowel joining blocks	4 (Timber)	1.9 × 1.9 × 0.6 cm $\frac{3}{4} \times \frac{3}{4} \times \frac{1}{4}$ in

Carcase

1 First cut out the floor pieces (B) which are very simple because all the edges are square (see figure 8.2). You do need to cut the shape for the protruding steps out of the floors, which is done by cutting off the front outside corners, leaving an 8 cm (3⅛ in) wide protrusion of about 3.8 cm (1½ in). The steps are then cut into this protrusion.

2 Cut the walls. The tops of the side walls (A) are angled to follow the fall of the roof, but the front (D) and back walls (C) have angled top edges to them, again following the fall of the roof. It is these angled cuts along the top edges of the front and back walls which will be difficult to achieve if you don't have the right tools. You could use a small band-saw, on which the table can be tilted to allow you to cut an angled edge, or a tilted radial-arm saw, or you could cut the edge square and then plane it by hand, at an angle, until you get the right shape.

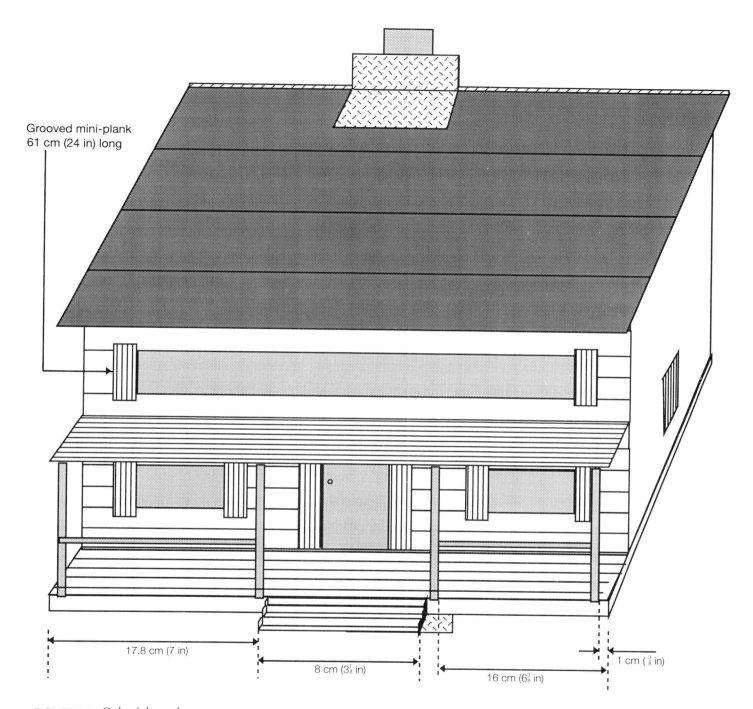

Grooved mini-plank
61 cm (24 in) long

17.8 cm (7 in)

8 cm (3⅛ in)

16 cm (6¾ in)

1 cm (⅜ in)

FIGURE 8.1 Colonial postbox

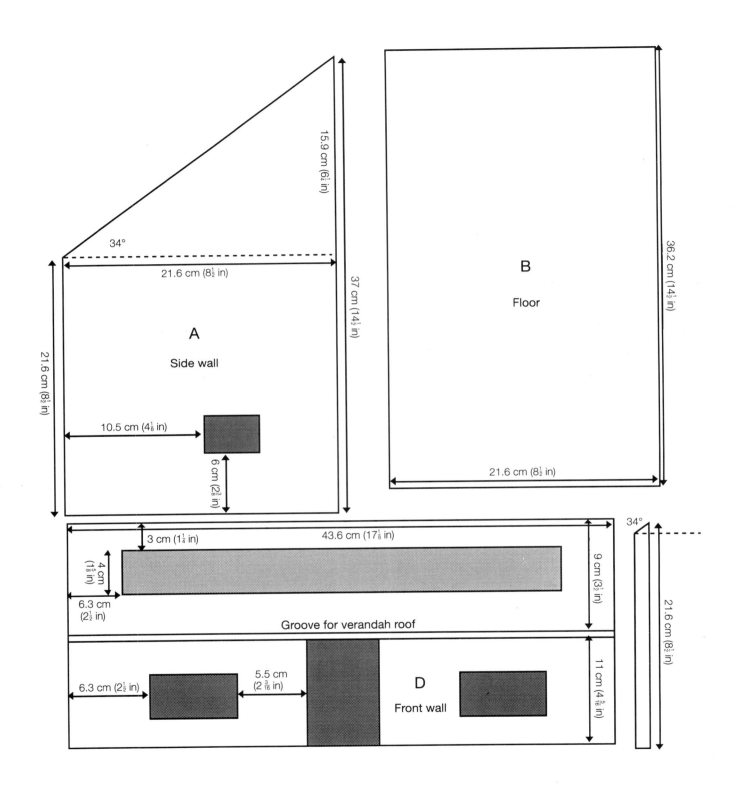

FIGURE 8.2 Colonial postbox: cutting patterns 1

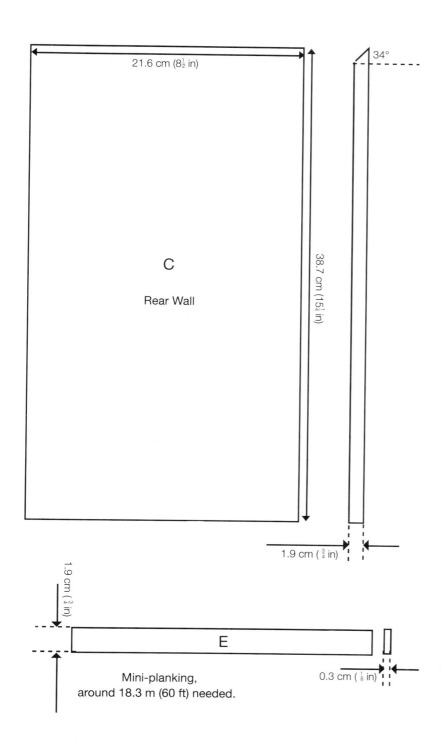

21.6 cm (8½ in)

34°

C

Rear Wall

38.7 cm (15¼ in)

1.9 cm (¾ in)

1.9 cm (¾ in)

E

Mini-planking,
around 18.3 m (60 ft) needed.

0.3 cm (⅛ in)

3 The front wall (D) also needs a slot cut in it for your letters to go in. Mark this out, then drilling a hole large enough to take your jigsaw blade. You can cut around the shape quite easily with either a power or a hand jigsaw.

4 Once you have all the pieces cut, you can start to assemble the carcase. All the joins are made by screwing and glueing the pieces together using a butt join. The screws' holes should be drilled and countersunk. The two rear wall pieces (C) are fixed together with the joining piece running all the way up the middle. Leave enough showing above the top of the walls for cutting the chimney shape.

5 Use screws through the top and bottom of the joining piece to fix the box on to the house or post. The top of the joining piece also acts as the chimney.

6 The side walls are then screwed on to the back walls, the angled top edge of the side walls should be flush with the lower angled edge of the top of the back walls. The bottoms of all of them should also be flush.

7 Screw and glue the floor pieces on to the bottoms of the back and side walls.

8 The front wall is then fixed in the same way on to the front of the structure, and the carcase is complete.

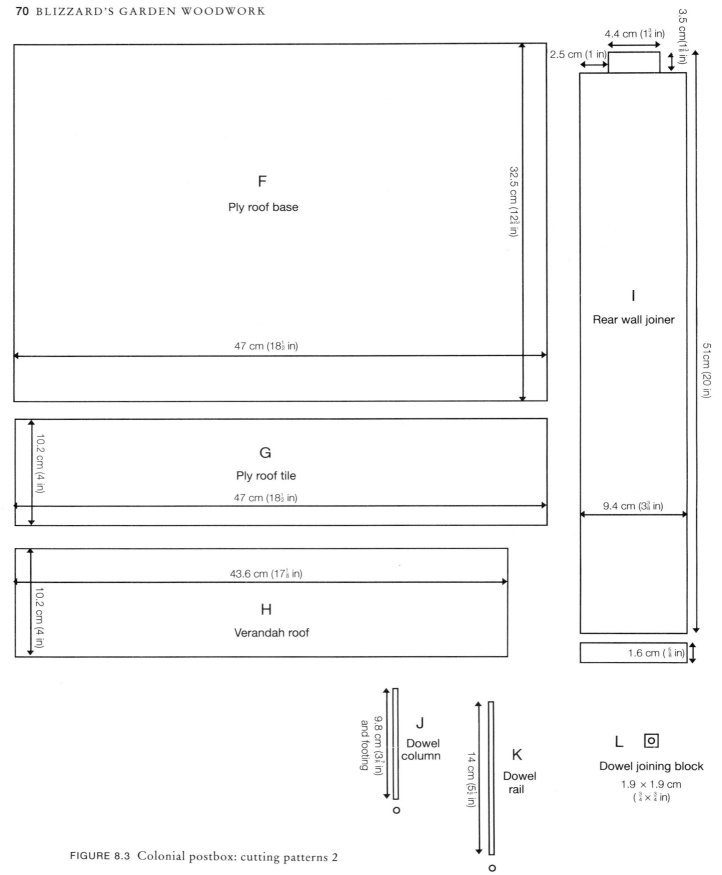

F

Ply roof base

32.5 cm (12¾ in)

47 cm (18½ in)

G

Ply roof tile

10.2 cm (4 in)

47 cm (18½ in)

43.6 cm (17⅛ in)

H

Verandah roof

10.2 cm (4 in)

4.4 cm (1¾ in)

3.5 cm (1⅜ in)

2.5 cm (1 in)

I

Rear wall joiner

51 cm (20 in)

9.4 cm (3⅜ in)

1.6 cm (⅝ in)

9.8 cm (3⅞ in)
and footing

J

Dowel
column

14 cm (5½ in)

K

Dowel
rail

L

Dowel joining block

1.9 × 1.9 cm
(¾ × ¾ in)

FIGURE 8.3 Colonial postbox: cutting patterns 2

Roof

1 The roof is made out of ply wood. First cut a piece to act as a base for the 'tiles', which is large enough to cover the whole of the top of the carcase with 2.5 cm (1 in) or so overhang all round. (See figure 8.3.)

2 Cut strip 'tiles' the full width of the roof. Into these tiles cut a pattern on the lower edge, apart from the one which will fit flush with the lower edge of the ply base. The pattern can be any shape to suit your personal taste.

3 The tiles are then pinned and glued on to the base starting at the bottom and allowing a generous overlap, and spaced evenly up the roof.

4 Fit a length of roofing felt between the top tile and the base, which tacks down to the rear wall when the roof is fitted. This stops water getting into the box from the top.

5 The roof is then fitted on to the carcase with a pair of hinges, surface mounted, between the top of the ply base and the angled top of the carcase back wall. You'll find you need to cut away a section of the roof top edge and the felt where it fouls the chimney on opening.

6 Cover this section by tacking a further piece of felt to act as 'flashing' for the chimney breast. If you tack it at the top and let it hang down it will also cover your top fixing point when you hang the box on a wall or post.

Planking

1 Cut the planking out of lengths of 2.5 cm (1 in) timber using a bench saw to 'slice' the planks off the edge. You could achieve the same using a band-saw, or even a hand-held circular saw.

2 Treat the planks with a quick-drying wood stain and preservative, on one side only since the other side is to be glued on to the carcase.

3 Draw the outline of the door and windows on the carcase and treat them with a dark colour stain.

4 Then plank up all around, cutting the planks to length and fitting them around the windows, doors and the verandah roof groove.

5 Make some 'shutters' to fit on to the doors and windows, which also helps to give a colonial feel to the box, from untreated planking with grooves cut down them to give a shutter look.

6 Cut down some planking to size to plank up the steps.

7 Finally, tack on some 'shut' shuttering on the side walls to give the impression of further windows there. If you can't be bothered with the planking you can paint them on, or cut lines along to simulate the edges of each plank, or combine the two.

Verandah

1 The roof of the verandah is a piece of ply cut to size and located into the groove in the front wall. It slopes slightly down to the front, where it is supported by four dowel columns. Drill the appropriate size holes in the front of the verandah floor 1.3 cm ($\frac{1}{2}$ in) deep, to locate the bottom of the dowels.

2 Locate the tops on to the front edge of the roof using small square blocks of wood again with the appropriate sized hole drilled through them. Achieve this by drilling down into a square 1.9 cm ($\frac{3}{4}$ in) batten and then cutting the blocks off the end.

3 The dowels and roof are then glued into position.

4 Finally, glue in the front rails.

Haywain

This small wagon is a miniature of the old style farm hay cart, and is made entirely using sawn timber (not planed) to give a rustic effect. It looks lovely standing in the garden with plant pots on it.

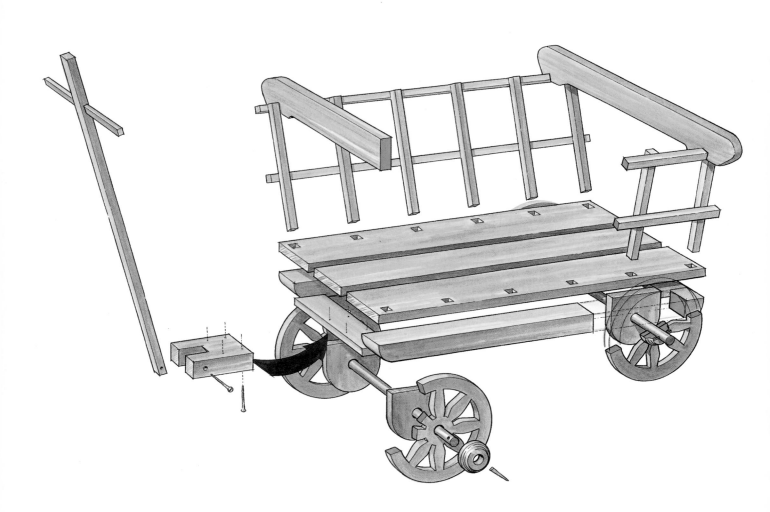

Tools and materials

- Pencil
- Flexible rule
- Set square
- Saw
- Jigsaw or coping saw
- Glass-paper
- Drill
- Countersink bit
- Screwdriver
- Chisel
- Mallet
- 3 doz 3 cm (1¼ in) No. 8 screws
- 300 ml pack waterproof glue
- Water-based wood stain preservative

Timber cutting list

Part	Quantity	Dimensions (L × W × Th)
Planks for wagon bed	3 (Planking)	91.4 × 15.2 × 1.9 cm 36 × 6 × ¾ in
Cross planks	2 (Planking)	35.6 × 7.6 × 1.9 cm 14 × 3 × ¾ in
'Chassis'	3 (Timbers)	91.4 × 5.1 × 5.1 cm 36 × 2 × 2 in
Axle bearers	4 (Planking)	15.2 × 15.2 × 1.9 cm 6 × 6 × ¾ in
Axle dowels	2 (Dowelling)	57 × 2.5 cm 22½ × 1 in
Wheels	4 (Shuttering)	15.2 cm 6 in
Hubs	4 (1.6 cm (⅝ in) timber ply)	4.2 cm × 1.6 cm 1⅝ × ⅝ in
Wheel wedges	4	To fit hole in axle
Fence verticals	12 (Timber)	40.2 × 2.5 × 1.9 cm 15³⁄₁₆ × 1 × ¾ in
Fence middle horizontals	2 (Timber)	87.8 × 2.5 × 1.9 cm 34½ × 1 × ¾ in
Fence top horizontals	2 (Timber)	37.6 × 2.5 × 1.9 cm 13⅝ × 1 × ¾ in
Fence cross-yokes	2 (Shaped timber)	72.6 × 2.5 × 1.9 cm 28⁹⁄₁₆ × 1 × ¾ in
Handle	1 (Timber)	91.4 × 3.5 × 3 cm 36 × 1⅜ × 1¼ in
Handle cross-piece	1 (Timber)	31.8 × 2.5 × 1.9 cm 12½ × 1 × ¾ in
Handle mounting block	1 (Timber)	15.2 × 10.2 × 5.1 cm 6 × 4 × 2 in

Construction

This haywain is ornamental and is not designed to be wheeled about as a trailer – the wheels and axles would have to be more substantial for that.

Wagon bed and chassis

1 The bed of the wagon is very simple. (See figure 9.1.) Hold together the three planks by screwing and glueing the two cross-planks underneath. Strengthen this by screwing and glueing two 'chassis' beams down the long edges of the bed and underneath.

2 The axle bearers at each corner (see figure 9.2) are made from the same planking as the bed with one round end and one square end. Holes, 2.5 cm (1 in) in diameter are drilled through the round ends to take the 2.5 cm (1 in) dowel rod axles. Then screw and glue the bearers on to the chassis beam at each corner of the wagon bed.

3 The slightly trickier bits are the holes that have to be cut out of the edge planks of the bed for the fences which are made of battening. Cut all the verticals first with a 10 degree mitre on each end. This is what gives the outward lean to the

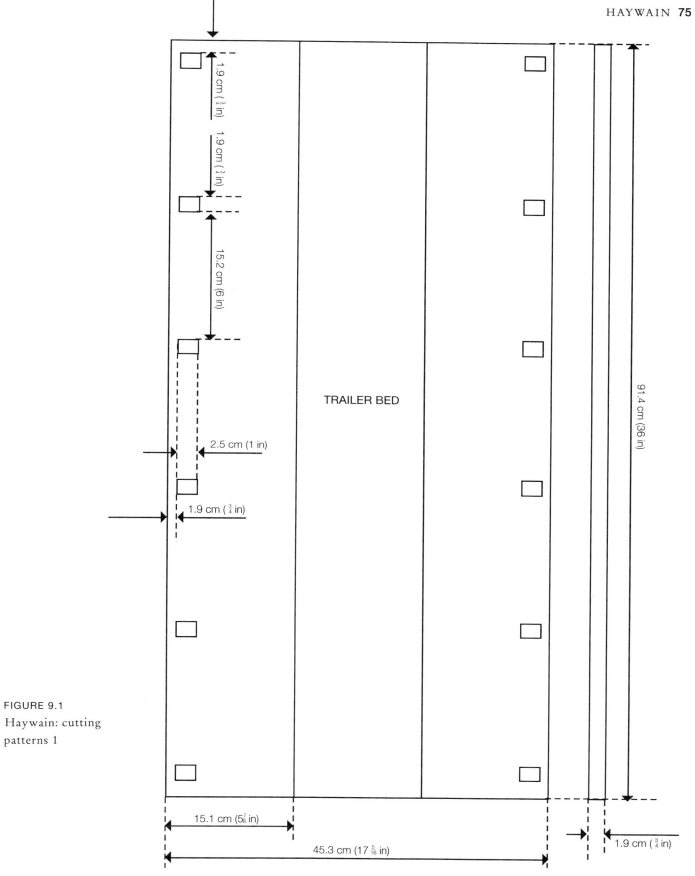

FIGURE 9.1
Haywain: cutting
patterns 1

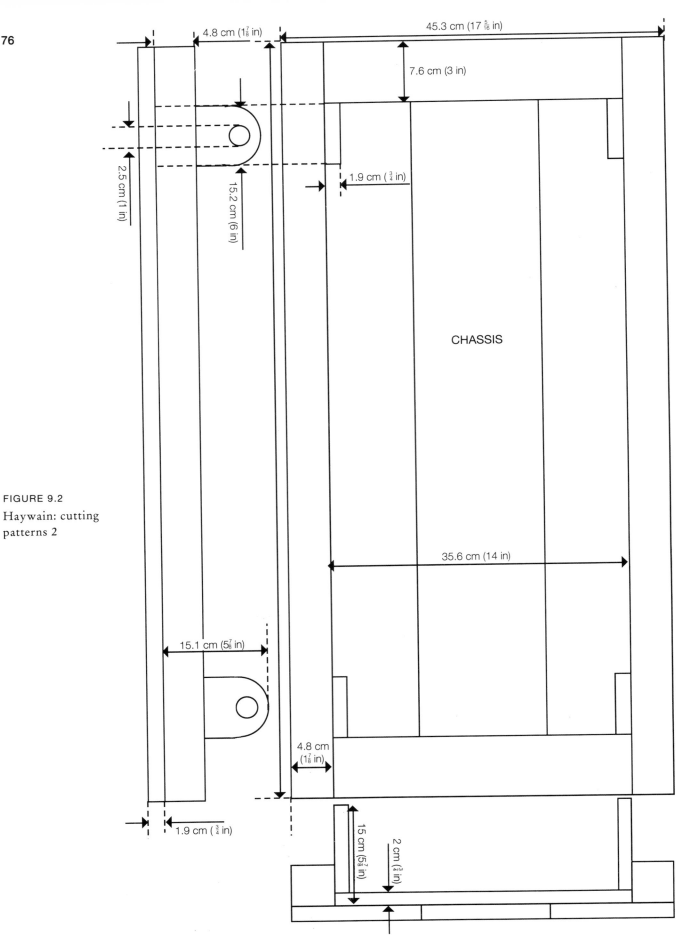

4.8 cm (1⅞ in)

45.3 cm (17 5/16 in)

7.6 cm (3 in)

2.5 cm (1 in)

15.2 cm (6 in)

1.9 cm (¾ in)

CHASSIS

35.6 cm (14 in)

15.1 cm (5⅞ in)

FIGURE 9.2
Haywain: cutting
patterns 2

4.8 cm
(1⅞ in)

1.9 cm (¾ in)

15 cm (5⅞ in)

2 cm (¾ in)

fences. Use the end of one of them to draw around at each position down the edge of the bed planks.

4 Then drill through the middle of the drawn shape at an angle of 10 degrees.

5 Draw the same shape on the other side centred on the drill's exit point. This gives the entry and exit of a batten 'driven' through the plank at 10 degrees.

6 You will need something to hold the plank firmly while you are chiselling in at an angle, otherwise the plank tends to 'walk' away from you as you work. Cut through the plank using a chisel and wooden mallet. Cut in from both sides to ensure clean straight edges on both sides of the plank.

7 Repeat this process until you have holes for six verticals on each side of the wagon's bed.

Fences

1 Put the verticals in position (see figure 9.3) and screw and glue the horizontal rails on. The ends of the middle rail are flush with the outer verticals, whereas the ends of the top rail protrude 2.5 cm (1 in) or so beyond to take the yoke that fits across between the fences.

2 Cut the cross-yokes, that connect the tops of the fences together, out of the same planking as the bed.

3 Draw the shape you want on the wood and cut around with a jigsaw, or you could use a coping saw.

4 Then offer the connecting cross-yokes up to the ends of the top horizontal battens and draw the shape of the batten ends on the yoke for the cut-outs.

5 Remove the wood from the cut-outs, which allows the yokes to sit down comfortably over the ends of the top horizontal battens of the fence. The bits of wood around the cut-out are quite vulnerable to breakage, and it can be a good idea to reinforce them with some ply. The fence is then complete.

Wheels

1 The wheels should be cut out of 1.9 cm ($\frac{3}{4}$ in) shuttering ply.

2 Draw the concentric circles for the hub and the rim on to the ply and then draw in the spokes using a template made up on stiff card.

3 Drill a hole in each section to be cut out to get the jigsaw blade in.

4 Use a jigsaw to cut out the wheels as solid pieces. You could theoretically do the whole thing by hand using a coping saw, but it is best to hire or buy an electric jigsaw.

5 Finally drill a 2.5 cm (1 in) diameter hole, using a flat bit, right through the centre to take the axle dowel.

6 Make the circular hubs out of some 1.6 cm ($\frac{5}{8}$ in) timber by drawing and cutting with the jigsaw in the same way.

7 Cut the axle dowels to length and drill holes through them to take the wedge-shaped wheel retainers.

Handle

1 The pulling handle is made from 3.8 cm ($1\frac{1}{2}$ in) timber. Cut a hole through one end to take the batten cross piece. Again drill and then cut through using a chisel in the same way as for the fence holes that you made in the cart's bed.

2 The mounting block is made by cutting a slanting channel through a block of wood at the angle required to give an upward slope to the handle when fitted. Again draw out the channel on the block and saw down the edges before cutting out the unwanted wood with a chisel.

3 Drill holes for the screws that hold the handle on and also the screws that hold the block on to the bottom of the front of the wagon bed.

4 You can achieve the same effect by cutting an angled block and screwing the handle on to it, and then screwing the block to the underside front of the cart.

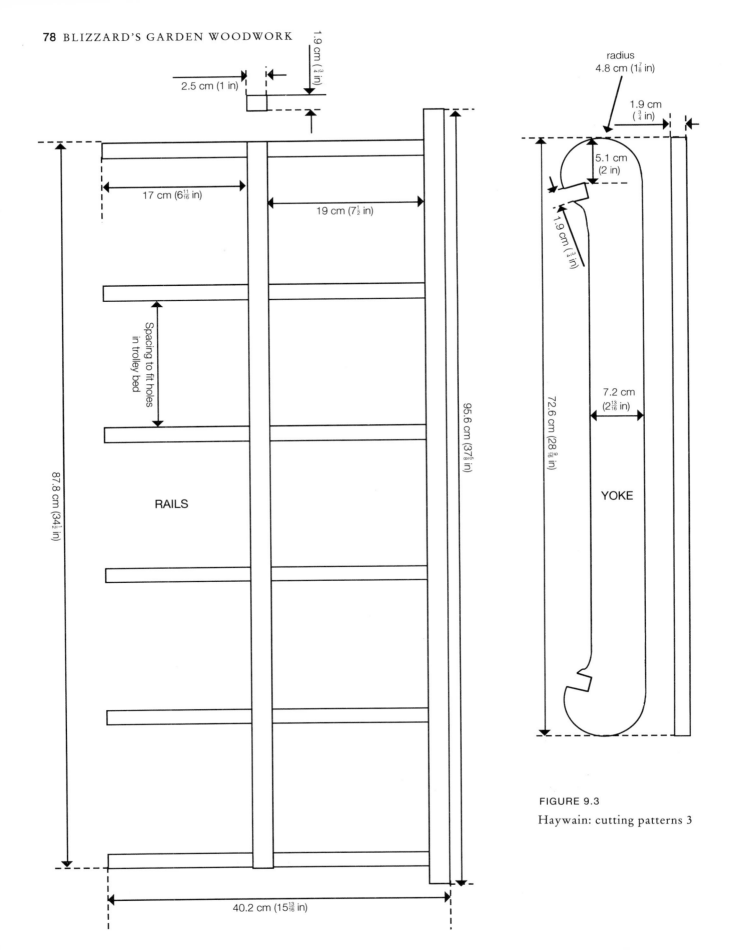

2.5 cm (1 in)

1.9 cm ($\frac{3}{4}$ in)

17 cm ($6\frac{11}{16}$ in)

19 cm ($7\frac{1}{2}$ in)

95.6 cm ($37\frac{5}{8}$ in)

Spacing to fit holes
in trolley bed

87.8 cm ($34\frac{1}{2}$ in)

RAILS

40.2 cm ($15\frac{13}{16}$ in)

radius
4.8 cm ($1\frac{7}{8}$ in)

1.9 cm
($\frac{3}{4}$ in)

5.1 cm
(2 in)

1.9 cm ($\frac{3}{4}$ in)

72.6 cm ($28\frac{9}{16}$ in)

7.2 cm
($2\frac{13}{16}$ in)

YOKE

FIGURE 9.3

Haywain: cutting patterns 3

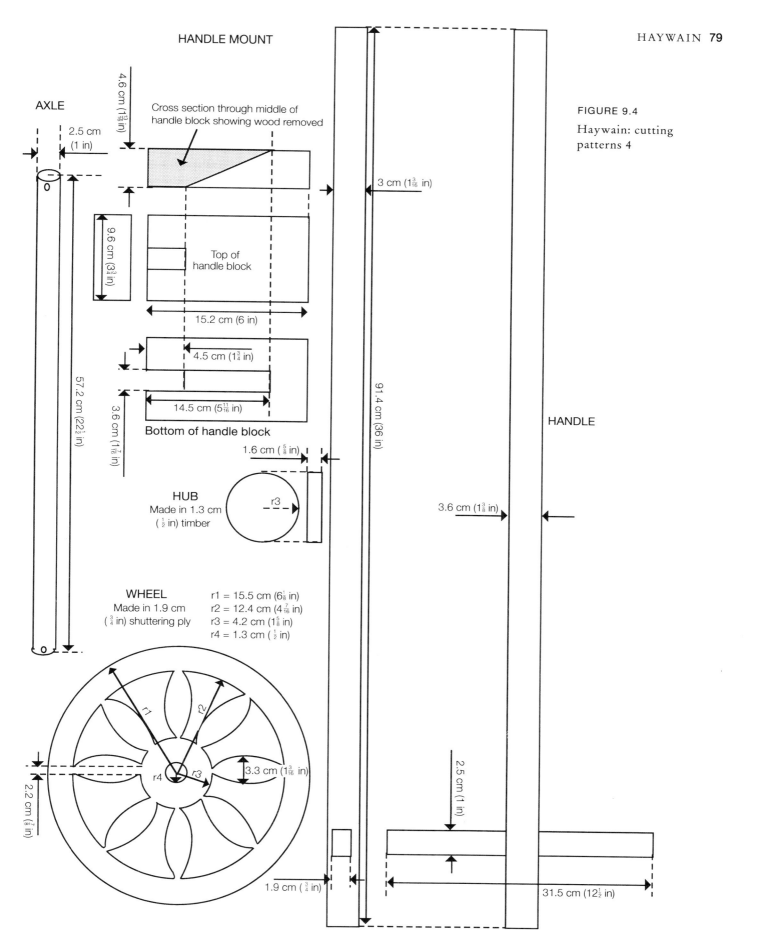

HANDLE MOUNT

AXLE

4.6 cm (1 13/16 in)

Cross section through middle of handle block showing wood removed

2.5 cm (1 in)

0

9.6 cm (3 3/4 in)

Top of handle block

15.2 cm (6 in)

57.2 cm (22 1/2 in)

4.5 cm (1 3/4 in)

3.6 cm (1 7/16 in)

14.5 cm (5 11/16 in)

Bottom of handle block

1.6 cm (5/8 in)

HUB
Made in 1.3 cm
(1/2 in) timber

r3

3 cm (1 3/16 in)

91.4 cm (36 in)

FIGURE 9.4

Haywain: cutting patterns 4

HANDLE

3.6 cm (1 3/8 in)

WHEEL
Made in 1.9 cm
(3/4 in) shuttering ply

r1 = 15.5 cm (6 1/8 in)
r2 = 12.4 cm (4 7/16 in)
r3 = 4.2 cm (1 5/8 in)
r4 = 1.3 cm (1/2 in)

r1

r2

r4 r3

3.3 cm (1 3/16 in)

2.2 cm (7/8 in)

2.5 cm (1 in)

1.9 cm (3/4 in)

31.5 cm (12 1/2 in)

Barbecue Trolley

It can seem an almost endless task, carrying all the barbecue things out to their temporary home in the garden. This two-wheeled barbecue trolley will make the whole process easier. It can be used by loading the two built-in trays in the kitchen and then wheeling the trolley to the barbecue, where it can act as a serving trolley for the food and drink when everything's ready. If you make it carefully and finish it well, it will even do for a kitchen trolley indoors when not in use in the garden!

Construction

The barbecue trolley has four legs and two rails – top and bottom. (See figure 10.1.) The legs can be shaped at the top either with bevelled edges and corners, or with a domed pyramid, if you draw the shape and plane off the bevels or cut with a tenon or coping saw. To give a flush finish the rails are set into the legs. The rebates for the rails must be cut into the legs accurately as they need to fit precisely. It is best to cut the rebates slightly too small (1 mm ($\frac{1}{32}$ in) or so), so that you can pare them out with a chisel to get an exact fit by forcing the rail into the rebate with a bit of a thump. If you are uncertain, practise on some spare bits of wood and you will soon get it right!

Each level of the trolley has fixed shelving and a removable tray. (See figure 10.2.)

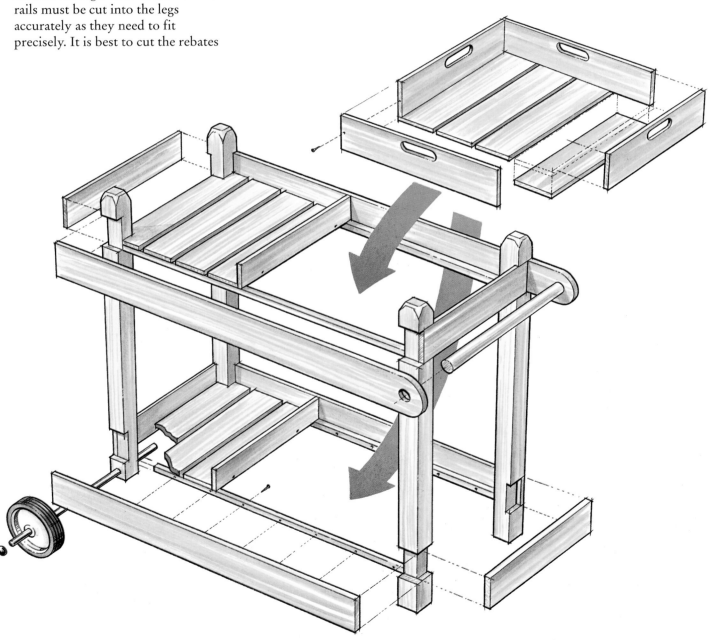

Tools and materials

- Pencil
- Flexible rule
- Set square
- Saw
- Jigsaw or coping saw
- Glass-paper
- Drill
- Countersink bit
- Screwdriver
- Chisel
- Wood mallet
- 5 doz 3.8 cm ($1\frac{1}{2}$ in) No. 8 screws
- 300 ml pack waterproof glue
- Water-based wood stain preservative
- 50.8 × 1 cm (20 × $\frac{3}{8}$ in) axle rod
- 2 15.2 cm (6 in) diameter wheels
- 2 1 cm ($\frac{3}{8}$ in) spring caps

Timber cutting list

Part	Quantity	Dimensions (L × W × Th)
Rear legs	2 (Planed timber)	91.4 × 5.1 × 5.1 cm 36 × 2 × 2 in
Wheeled legs	2 (Planed timber)	87.8 × 5.1 × 5.1 cm $34\frac{1}{2}$ × 2 × 2 in
Upper long rails	2 (Planed timber)	99 × 10.2 × 1.6 cm 39 × 4 × $\frac{5}{8}$ in
Lower long rails	2 (Planed timbers)	88.9 × 10.2 × 1.6 cm 35 × 4 × $\frac{5}{8}$ in
Short rails	4 (Planed timber)	42.5 × 10.2 × 1.6 cm $16\frac{3}{4}$ × 4 × $\frac{5}{8}$ in
Trolley handle	1 (Dowelling)	45.7 × 2.5 cm 18 × 1 in
Shelf supports	4 (Battens	81.3 cm (32 in)
Top tray slats and end frame	6 (Planed timber)	42.5 × 10.2 × 1.6 cm $16\frac{3}{4}$ × 4 × $\frac{5}{8}$ in
Top tray side frame	2 (Planed timber)	37 × 10.2 × 1.6 cm $14\frac{1}{2}$ × 4 × $\frac{5}{8}$ in
Top shelf slats and fiddle	5 (Planed timber)	42.5 × 10.2 × 1.6 cm $16\frac{3}{4}$ × 4 × $\frac{5}{8}$ in
Bottom shelf slats and fiddle	4 (Planed timber)	42.5 × 10.2 × 1.6 cm $16\frac{3}{4}$ × 4 × $\frac{5}{8}$ in
Bottom tray slats and end frame	7 (Planed timber)	42.5 × 10.2 × 1.6 cm $16\frac{3}{4}$ × 4 × $\frac{5}{8}$ in
Bottom tray side frame	2 (Planed timber)	47 × 10.2 × 1.6 cm $18\frac{1}{2}$ × 4 × $\frac{5}{8}$ in

Cutting the rebates

1 Lay two legs side by side and place the next two on top. Line the ends up and tape them together, and draw a line with a rule all the way round the outside of the four legs. (See figure 2.2.) This marks the sides that are going to have the rebates cut in them.

2 Take the tape off and lay all the legs out on a flat surface side by side with one pencil-marked side uppermost. To get the rebates on all the legs at the same level clamp or

tape them together having made sure the tops and bottoms line up, and mark them up all together. Place a top rail on the legs positioned at the correct level and use a set square to make sure it is facing at right-angles to the legs and, using the rail as a rule, mark across the legs in pencil, both above and below the rail.

3 Try to keep your pencil mark as tight into the rail as you can, so that when you go to cut the rebate out, the rail will fit tightly into it. Then repeat this procedure for the lower rail.

4 If you now untape and turn the legs so that the other pencilled sides are showing, you can mark up the rebates in the same way on the other side.

5 The easiest method to mark the depth of the rebate on the sides of the legs, so that you know exactly how deep to cut into the leg, is to place a rail on end where it will eventually fit, and then draw around it on to the side of the leg. Again make sure you keep your pencil marks in very close to the rail end so that the fit will be tight.

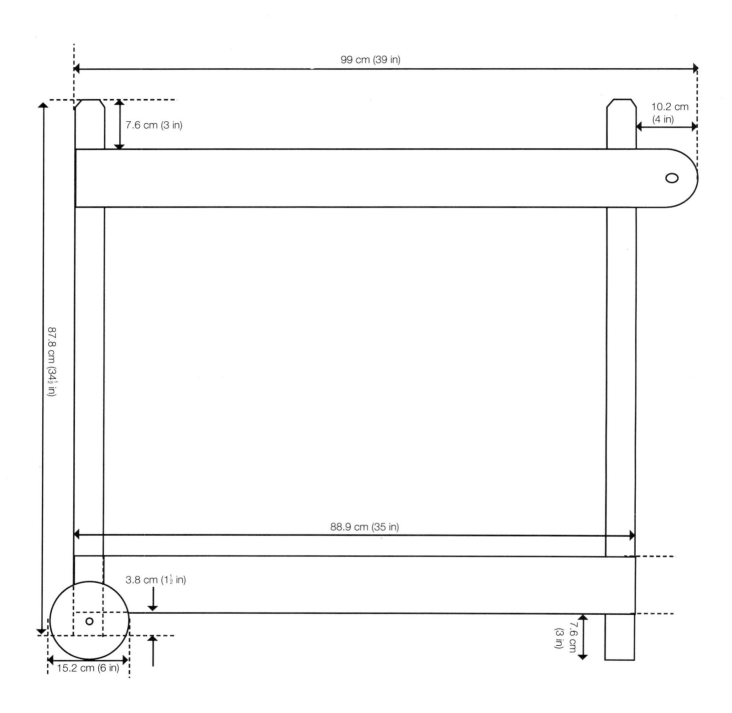

FIGURE 10.1 Barbecue trolley: cutting patterns 1

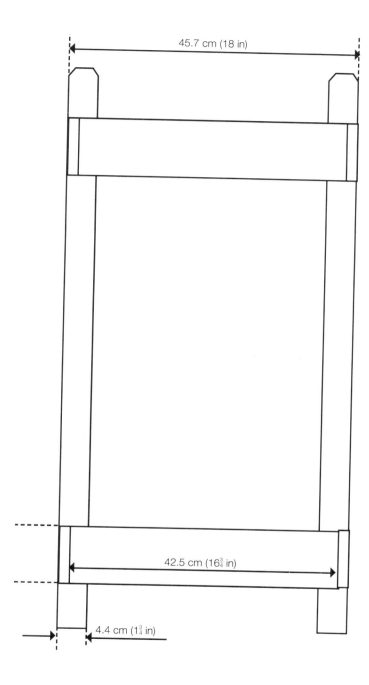

45.7 cm (18 in)

42.5 cm (16¾ in)

4.4 cm (1¾ in)

6 Cut out one of the rebates first and check to see the rail fits tightly before doing the others. Cut the wood down the lines to the depth marked, and then chisel out the wood in small chunks, rather than trying to take the whole depth out at one go. When you get down close to the depth mark, work in from both sides towards the middle to avoid splitting the wood as you chisel. Complete all the other rebates on the legs after checking the first one.

Glueing up the frame

1 Work on a large flat surface. First assemble one long side of the frame dry (i.e. without any glue). Check that the frame is square by checking the diagonals of the rectangular space between the lower and the middle rails are equal.

2 When it fits together well, take it apart and apply wood glue.

3 Reassemble, check the diagonal again, and apply pressure to the joints using 'G' clamps or weights to hold it all together while you work and while the glue sets.

4 Leave to set and assemble the other long side in the same way.

5 When both are set, assemble the whole structure by fitting the short side rails across between the two frames already built.

6 Check they all fit properly and take apart for glueing.

7 Glue up and assemble. Remember to check the diagonals on the short sides for squareness. It is often easiest to do all this while standing the whole structure on a flat floor.

Shelves

1 Half of each level of the trolley is made up of fixed shelving, and half is a removable tray. Make the fixed shelf slats all the same length, with eight slats to each of the shelves. It is easiest to treat your barbecue trolley before fitting the slats. You can treat all the slats together on the flat, turn them, and get to the edges easily. It also makes the frame easier to treat. You can paint it with colours of your choice or use one of the water-based stain preservatives. Whatever you choose check that it is suitable for a food trolley.

2 Support the slots by screwing and glueing battens to the bottom edge of the long side rails.

3 Fit a fiddle – an edge piece to keep things from falling off the shelf when the trays are not in place – by simply screwing and glueing another slat to the edge of the last slat in the shelf.

4 Make trays to fit in the other halves, one on the top and one on the bottom, from shelf slats, with the same sort of timber fitted around the edges to act as a fiddle. The top tray is made from four slats. On the lower shelf make a slightly larger tray, using five slats. These trays are useful for carrying the food, drink, plates and cutlery to your barbecue area.

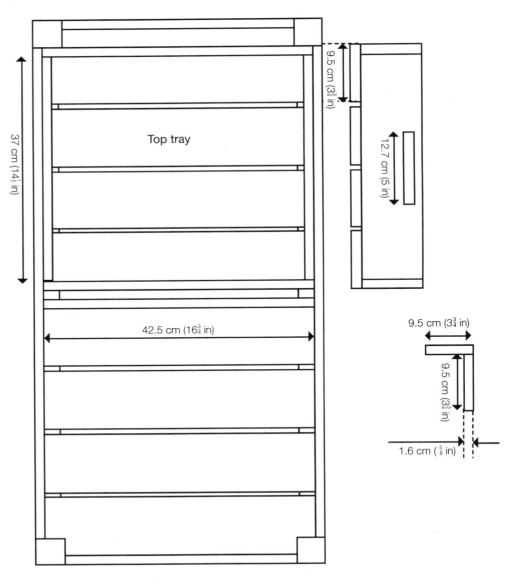

Upper level

FIGURE 10.2 Barbecue trolley: cutting patterns 2

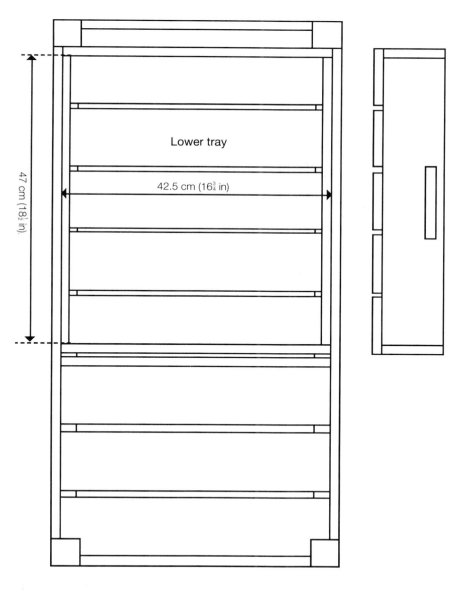

47 cm (18½ in)

Lower tray

42.5 cm (16¾ in)

Lower level

Hammock Stand

No matter how many trees you have in your garden, there are never two trees at the right distance apart to sling a hammock between. This design for a hammock stand allows you to put your hammock anywhere you like in the garden. It is made in two halves so that if you have one good tree in a suitable place you can just build half the stand and tie the other end of your hammock to your tree.

Construction

The stand is made out of 22.9 cm (9 in) × 3.1cm (1¼ in) planed timber (PSE). It is constructed in two identical halves (see figure 11.1) which are then joined in the middle by a joining box. If you need only one end, build half and put a short piece across the end of the central beam nearest the tree to dig in and prevent the stand moving towards the tree when you swing in your hammock.

The key parts of the structure are laminated using three pieces of timber. Many of the parts are shaped to give the stand its curved, almost nautical appearance. (See figure 11.2.)

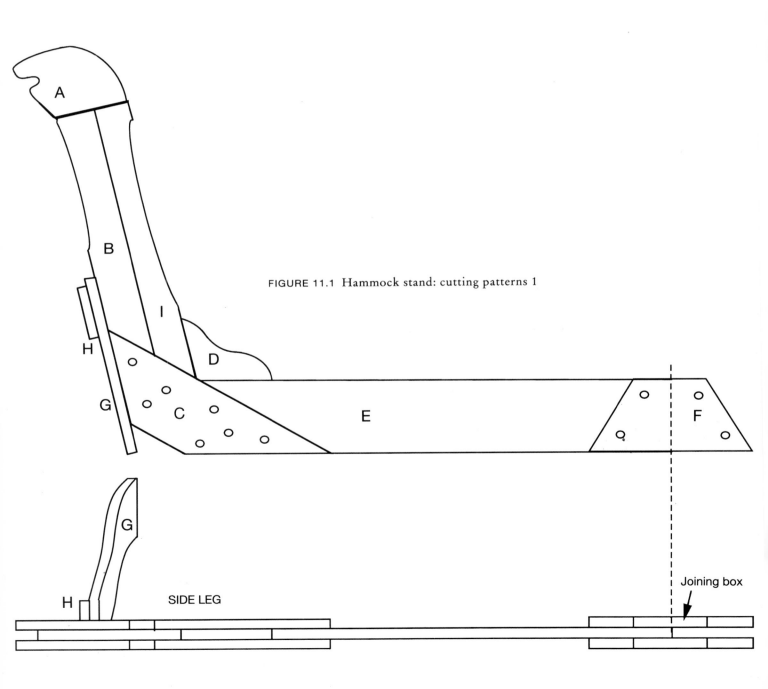

FIGURE 11.1 Hammock stand: cutting patterns 1

SIDE LEG

Joining box

Tools and materials

- Pencil
- Flexible rule
- Set square
- Saw
- Jigsaw
- Drill
- Countersink bit
- Screwdriver
- Spanners
- Glass paper
- Sander
- Spoke shave
- 5 doz 4.4 cm ($1\frac{3}{4}$ in) No. 8 screws
- 300 ml pack waterproof glue
- 1 doz 10 × 100 mm ($\frac{3}{8}$ × $3\frac{7}{8}$ in) coach bolts
- 6.3 cm ($2\frac{1}{2}$ in) No. 10 screws
- Hammock
- Circular straps
- 3 cm ($1\frac{3}{16}$ in) dowel cut to length
- Two-part wood filler
- Water-based wood stain preservative

Timber cutting list (Shapes as on figure 11.2)

Part	Quantity	Dimensions (L × W × Th)
Head cheek blocks	4 (Timber)	31 × 22.9 × 3.1 cm ($12\frac{3}{16}$ × 9 × $1\frac{1}{4}$ in)
Upright stiffeners	4 (Timber)	71.8 × 22.9 × 3.1 cm ($28\frac{1}{4}$ × 9 × $1\frac{1}{4}$ in)
Upright to keel joining blocks	4 (Timber)	74.5 × 22.9 × 3.1 cm ($29\frac{5}{16}$ × 9 × $1\frac{1}{4}$ in)
Upright support knees	2 (Timber)	23.3 × 22.9 × 3.1 cm ($9\frac{3}{16}$ × 9 × $1\frac{1}{4}$ in)
Keels	2 (Timber)	190 × 22.9 × 3.1 cm ($74\frac{1}{8}$ × 9 × $1\frac{1}{4}$ in)
Keel joining blocks	2 (Timber)	58 × 22.9 × 3.1 cm ($22\frac{3}{16}$ × 9 × $1\frac{1}{4}$ in)
Lateral feet	4 (Timber)	65 × 22.9 × 3.1 cm ($25\frac{2}{16}$ × 9 × $1\frac{1}{4}$ in)
Foot joining blocks	2 (Timber)	22 × 22.9 × 3.1 cm ($8\frac{11}{16}$ × 9 × $1\frac{1}{4}$ in)
Uprights	2 (Timber)	130 × 22.9 × 3.1 cm ($51\frac{3}{16}$ × 9 × $1\frac{1}{4}$ in)

Cutting

1 Mark all the shapes needed on the wood and cut out, ideally using a jigsaw or a band saw. If you haven't got one of these it is a good idea to hire one for the job. It will be a lot of work with a hand coping saw! The actual curves do not need to be exact as long as the pieces fit together. The rest are straight cuts and can be done using any saw. Use a powered saw of some sort if you can as 22.9 cm (9in) × 3.1 cm ($1\frac{1}{4}$ in) timber is substantial and you will need a lot of muscle to cut it by hand.

2 The top edges of these bits will need to be champhered off so they are not sharp. For this use a spoke shave.

Assembling

1 Once you have cut all the bits, assemble the head section (see figure 11.3) and clamp it together.

2 Drill and counter sink for the screws which must be at least 4.4 cm ($1\frac{3}{4}$ in) no. 8s.

3 Glue and screw the head section together. Note that the head cheek blocks are higher than the top of the upright which provides a channel for the hammock attachment straps to run in.

4 Assemble and clamp the side stiffeners.

5 Again drill and counter sink.

6 Glue up and screw the stiffeners into position.

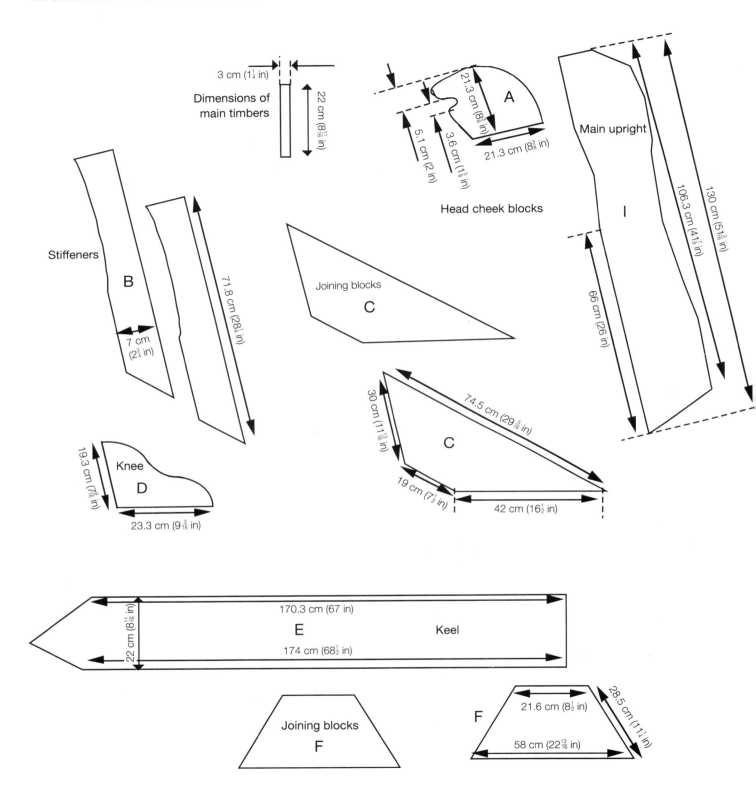

3 cm (1¼ in)

Dimensions of
main timbers

22 cm (8¹¹⁄₁₆ in)

21.3 cm (8⅜ in)

A

5.1 cm (2 in)

3.6 cm (1¹³⁄₁₆ in)

21.3 cm (8⅜ in)

Head cheek blocks

Main upright

106.3 cm (41⅞ in)

130 cm (51³⁄₁₆ in)

I

Stiffeners

B

71.8 cm (28¼ in)

Joining blocks

C

7 cm
(2¾ in)

66 cm (26 in)

19.3 cm (7⁹⁄₁₆ in)

Knee
D

23.3 cm (9³⁄₁₆ in)

30 cm (11¹³⁄₁₆ in)

74.5 cm (29⁵⁄₁₆ in)

C

19 cm (7½ in)

42 cm (16½ in)

170.3 cm (67 in)

E   Keel

22 cm (8¹¹⁄₁₆ in)

174 cm (68½ in)

Joining blocks

F

21.6 cm (8½ in)

28.5 cm (11¼ in)

F

58 cm (22¹³⁄₁₆ in)

FIGURE 11.2 Hammock stand: cutting patterns 2

7 Position and clamp the upright to the keel-joining blocks. Drill holes for the screws and screw into position.

8 Fit the keel and clamp into position. Drill bolt holes and bolt together using coach bolts. The coach bolts will need to be substantial – 10 cm (3⅞ in) by 1 cm (⅜ in) diameter. These are used so that you can take the stand to bits for winter storage. If you don't need it to come to bits then you can use screws and glue on all the joints. In the joints where you use coach bolts you will need to use 6.3 cm (2½ in) No. 10 screws.

9 Position the support knee, and glue it to the keel only. This will allow you to disassemble the keel from the upright for easier storage.

10 Put the two feet together in position and clamp the joining block onto them. Drill and countersink all the holes. The outer screws hold the two feet together, while the inner ones are larger and attach the feet to the upright.

11 Position and clamp the keel-joining blocks, that join the two halves of the keel together, on the end of the keel as shown, and drill the bolt holes. You can glue them on to one of the keel halves if you wish, leaving the other side unglued so that you can disassemble the keel length for storage.

12 Place the keel on a flat surface with the upright in the air. Get a friend to hold the whole structure while you clamp and drill the feet in position. Screw the feet on. If you want to be able to take the feet off, don't use glue.

The second half

1 Repeat the process again for the other half.

2 When you are ready, put the two halves together with the keel ends sandwiched by the joining blocks and drill holes for the last two bolts in the keel-joining block. Bolt them in and the main structural work is done.

Finishing

1 Fill over all the screw heads with two part wood-filler, which can be sanded flat and stained like wood, to give a really nice finish.

2 Spend some time with a sander and spoke-shave finishing off all the surfaces ready for treating.

3 I use a water-based preservative stain. There are a whole range of colours to suit all tastes.

Attaching the hammock

Attach the hammock to the structure at each end using continuous circular straps. These go through the loop in the end of the hammock and loop through themselves. At the other end they go round a length of 3 cm (1³⁄₁₆ in) dowel rod. This dowel fits neatly into the mouth in the head of the upright and is kept in position by the tension on the strap. You may find a different way, but the recess in the head is designed to take a 3 cm (1³⁄₁₆ in) dowel rod which must be joined to the hammock in some way.

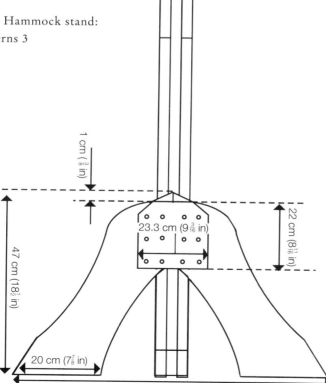

FIGURE 11.3 Hammock stand: cutting patterns 3

Head cheek blocks

1 cm (⅜ in)

23.3 cm (9³⁄₁₆ in)

22 cm (8¹¹⁄₁₆ in)

47 cm (18½ in)

20 cm (7⅞ in)

106 cm (41¾ in)

Storage Bench

This useful bench doubles as an easy seat and as a storage space for 'wet' garden gear such as wellingtons, plant pots, and non-rusting tools. It is designed to let rainwater drain through the storage box and the slots between the planks on all four sides, and the seat and the bottom allow the air through to dry off implements when wet.

Construction

The bench is constructed around the four legs. The box of the bench is built by screwing planks on the sides, leaving short legs protruding all around underneath and backrest supports up the back. The backrest itself is inset into the top of the back legs. The base of the box rests on pieces of batten, which are screwed and glued to the bottom edge of the lowest side planks. The seat, formed using two planks held together by two crosspieces, is hinged on to a narrow plank fixed along the back of the top of the box.

All screws, apart from the hinge screws, should be countersunk, so drill countersunk holes for them. Pilot holes should be drilled into the wood the screws are fixed into.

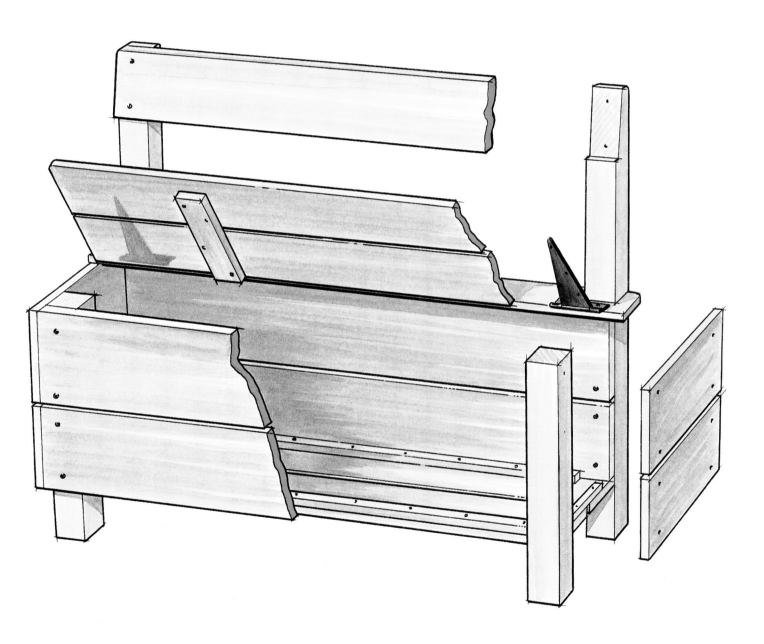

Tools and materials

- Pencil
- Flexible rule
- Set square
- Saw
- Drill
- Countersink bit
- Screwdriver
- Plane
- Chisel
- Wood mallet
- 5 doz 3 cm (1¼ in) No. 8 screws (black-jappaned, round-headed)
- 300 ml pack waterproof glue
- 2 'T' hinges
- Water-based wood stain preservative

Timber cutting list

Part	Quantity	Dimensions (L × W × Th)
Seat back rest	1 (Planed timber)	91.4 × 15.2 × 1.9 cm 36 × 6 × ¾ in
Seat top planks	2 (Planed timber)	91.4 × 15.2 × 1.9 cm 36 × 6 × ¾ in
Seat top plank fixing strip	2 (Timber)	24.8 × 7.6 × 1.9 cm 9¾ × 3 × ¾ in
Box front planks	2 (Timber)	86.4 × 15.2 × 1.9 cm 34 × 6 × ¾ in
Box back planks	2 (Timber)	86.4 × 15.2 × 1.9 cm 34 × 6 × ¾ in
Box side planks	4 (Timber)	38.1 × 15.2 × 1.9 cm 15 × 6 × ¾ in
Box bottom planks	2 (Timber)	86.4 × 15.2 × 1.9 cm 34 × 6 × ¾ in
Seat rear fixed plank	1 (Planed timber)	91.4 × 10.5 × 1.9 cm 36 × 4⅛ × ¾ in
Front legs	2 (Timber)	40.6 × 5.1 × 5.1 cm 16 × 2 × 2 in
Back legs	2 (Timber)	81.3 × 5.1 × 5.1 cm 32 × 2 × 2 in
Floor fixing battens (long side)	2 (Battening)	71.2 × 2.5 × 1.9 cm 28 × 1 × ¾ in
Floor fixing battens (long side)	2 (Battening)	30.5 × 2.5 × 1.9 cm 12 × 1 × ¾ in

Cutting

1 The first step is to make up and cut all your timber pieces to length. (See figure 12.1.)

2 Plane a chamfer around the bottom of all four sides of each leg. This will stop the timber splitting out as you drag it from place to place around the garden.

3 Cut the required inset into the top of the back legs to take the back rest. This produces an angle which makes the bench much more comfortable to sit on.

Assembly

1 The long sides of the bench box can then be screwed and glued into position on the front sides of the front and back legs – the top of the planks should be at the same height up from the bottom of the legs. To achieve this you can strap the legs together with tape and mark the level of the top of the front legs directly on to the longer back legs.

2 Remembering to leave a gap between the planks, screw the back planks of the box on to the front face of the back legs, leaving the back legs outside the box, the planks' ends finishing flush with the legs.

3 The front planks screw on to the front face of the front legs which leaves the front legs inside the box. Again the planks' ends finish flush with the legs.

4 Screw the side planks on to the legs and cover the ends of the front planks, and finish flush with the back of the back legs.

5 Screw and glue pieces of batten to the bottom of the bottom planks all round the inside of the box.

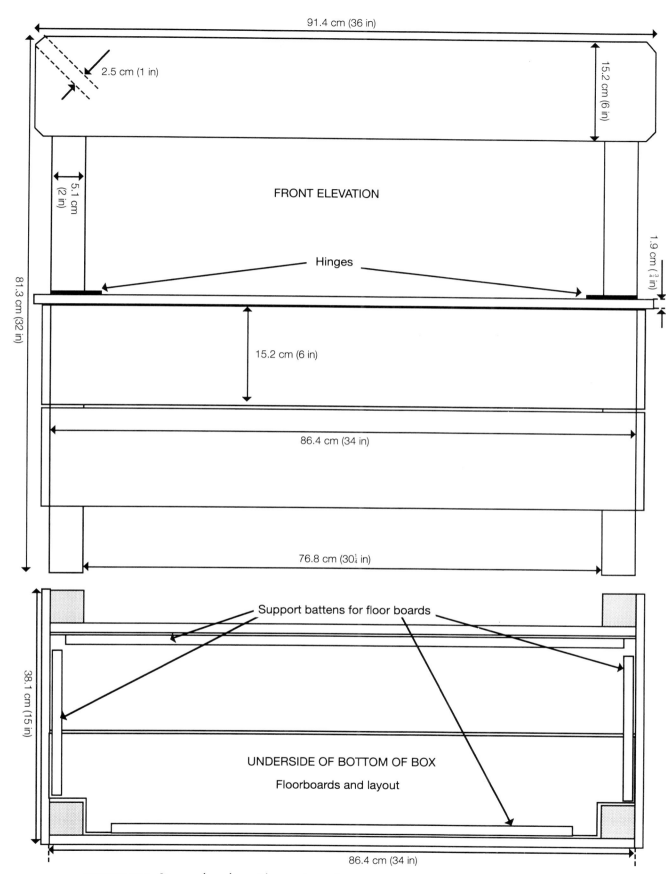

FIGURE 12.1 Storage bench: cutting patterns 1

6 Cut the base planks. Note that the front plank needs squares cut out of the corners, so that it fits around the front legs.

7 Screw the base planks into place – a single screw at each end should be sufficient for this.

Seat

1 The seat is formed from three planks. (See figure 12.2.) The rear one, which is screwed down to the top of the box, is narrower than the front two that form the lifting seat. Cut the rear plank to length.

2 Mark out and cut the recess holes that allow the rear plank to fit neatly around the back legs.

3 Fix the rear plank into position by screwing through into the tops of the back and side planks.

4 Cut a small facet into the corners of the back rest and the front plank of the lifting seat, to help take some of the squareness out of the design.

5 Cut the two lifting seat planks to length.

6 Join together the two lifting seat planks by two cross-members on which you have cut a champher to improve their look. The gap between the two planks should be the same as the gaps in the box planking.

7 The seat is then hinged on to the fixed back plank using black 'T' hinges and japanned round-headed screws.

8 Finally screw the back rest into place by using a single screw through from the back of the leg into the wood of the back rest. Cut a champher on the back of the top of the back legs.

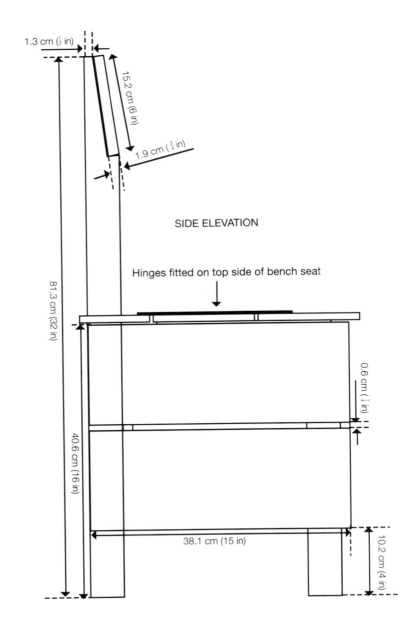

SIDE ELEVATION

Hinges fitted on top side of bench seat

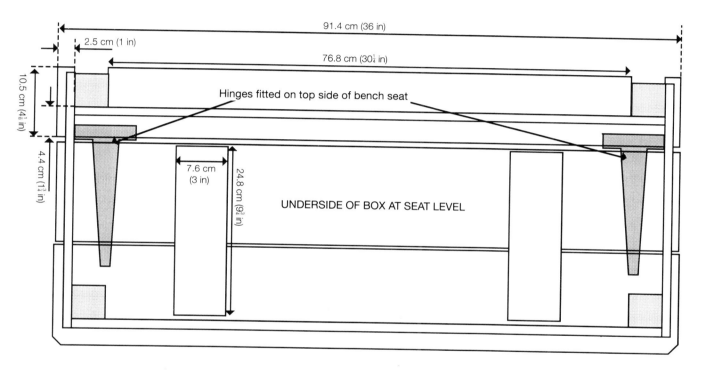

FIGURE 12.2 Storage bench: cutting patterns 2

Versailles Tub

This planter tub is designed with a tall trellis for climbing plants. The trellis is removable, so that you will also be able to use the planter as a container for other plants too.

Construction

There are no traditional woodworking joints involved, just glue and screws. Before you start, take time to study the cutting list and figures 13.1 and 13.2. A bit of time spent doing this will prevent mistakes later on.

Tools and materials

- Pencil
- Flexible rule
- Set square
- Saw
- Drill
- Countersink bit
- Screwdriver
- Plane
- 6 doz 3.8 cm ($1\frac{1}{2}$ in) No. 8 screws
- 300 ml pack waterproof glue
- Water-based wood stain preservative

Timber cutting list

Part	Quantity	Dimensions (L × W × Th)
Legs (pyramid topped version)	4 (Timber)	74.9 × 7.6 × 7.6 cm $29\frac{1}{2}$ × 3 × 3 in
Walls	16 (Tongue and groove 'V' board)	46.3 cm $18\frac{1}{4}$ in lengths
Wall fixing battens	8 (Battening)	45.7 × 2.5 × 2.5 cm 18 × 1 × 1 in
Floor fixing battens	2 (Battening)	46.3 × 2.5 × 2.5 cm $18\frac{1}{4}$ × 1 × 1 in
Trellis foot rest blocks	4 (Battening)	7.6 × 2.5 × 2.5 cm 3 × 1 × 1 in
Capping strips	4 (Timber)	46.3 × 7.6 × 1.6 cm $18\frac{1}{4}$ × 3 × $\frac{5}{8}$ in
Flooring	5 (Tongue and groove floor boarding)	54.6 cm $21\frac{1}{2}$ in lengths
Trellis uprights	4 (Battening)	101.6 × 2.5 × 1.9 cm 40 × 1 × $\frac{3}{4}$ in
Trellis north and south walls	2 (Battening)	10.2 × 2.5 × 1.9 cm 4 × 1 × $\frac{3}{4}$ in
Trellis north and south walls	2 (Battening)	17.8 × 2.5 × 1.9 cm 7 × 1 × $\frac{3}{4}$ in
Trellis north and south walls	2 (Battening)	24.1 × 2.5 × 1.9 cm $9\frac{1}{2}$ × 1 × $\frac{3}{4}$ in
Trellis north and south walls	2 (Battening)	30.5 × 2.5 × 1.9 cm 12 × 1 × $\frac{3}{4}$ in
Trellis north and south walls	2 (Battening)	38.1 × 2.5 × 1.9 cm 15 × 1 × $\frac{3}{4}$ in
Trellis north and south walls	2 (Battening)	45.7 × 2.5 × 1.9 cm 18 × 1 × $\frac{3}{4}$ in
Trellis east and west walls	2 (Battening)	5.1 × 2.5 × 1.9 cm 2 × 1 × $\frac{3}{4}$ in
Trellis east and west walls	2 (Battening)	12.7 × 2.5 × 1.9 cm 5 × 1 × $\frac{3}{4}$ in
Trellis east and west walls	2 (Battening)	19.1 × 2.5 × 1.9 cm $7\frac{1}{2}$ × 1 × $\frac{3}{4}$ in
Trellis east and west walls	2 (Battening)	25.4 × 2.5 × 1.9 cm 10 × 1 × $\frac{3}{4}$ in
Trellis east and west walls	2 (Battening)	33 × 2.5 × 1.9 cm 13 × 1 × $\frac{3}{4}$ in
Trellis east and west walls	2 (Battening)	40.6 × 2.5 × 1.9 cm 16 × 1 × $\frac{3}{4}$ in

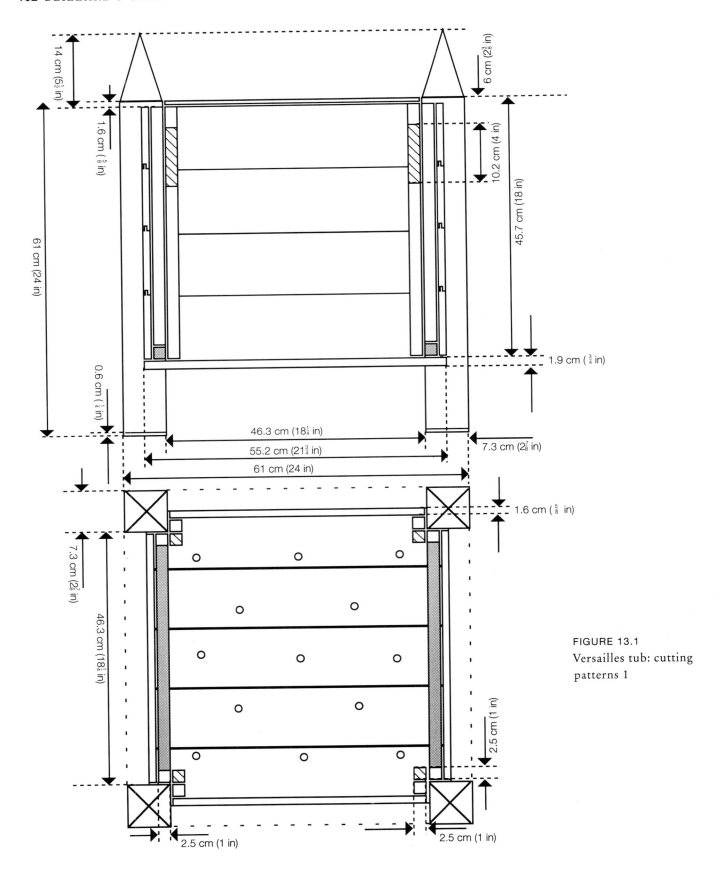

FIGURE 13.1
Versailles tub: cutting
patterns 1

Legs

1 The legs were made with a 'sharpened' pyramid on top. To make the sharp ended legs cut four legs to length, and mark up in pencil the areas to be sawn off the first two opposing sides.

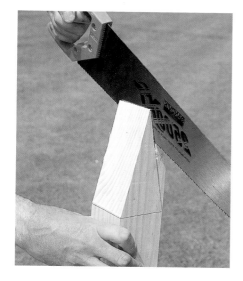

2 Put a leg in a vice or some other clamping device like a Workmate, and saw off one side of the pyramid, preferably with a tenon saw.

3 Then turn the leg over and do the other side. You then have a wedge shape.

4 Mark up on the sawn faces, the sections that need removing to complete the pyramid. Reclamp and saw them off.

5 Repeat this for all four legs.

6 Finally use a plane to make a 0.6 cm ($\frac{1}{4}$ in) chamfer around the bottom of the legs. This stops the wood splintering if you drag the box around later.

7 If you prefer you can square off each leg and screw a ready-made spherical or other shape into the top of each leg.

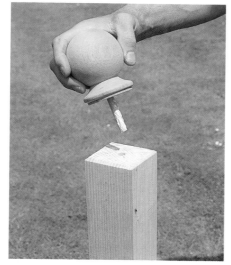

Making the box

1 Cut the wall fixing battens that are screwed on to the edges of the legs.

2 Drill pilot holes for the screws, or the battens may split.

3 Glue and screw the battens into place to give the strongest result.

4 The walls are made from standard tongue and groove 'V' boarding. The tongue on one board fits neatly into the groove on the next, leaving a 'V' indentation on one side of the boarding which provides a decorative feature for the walls. When cutting the boards make sure they are all the same length. This is most easily done by measuring and cutting the first one, and then using it to mark up each subsequent one.

5 Drill two pilot holes in each end of each board, 1.3 cm ($\frac{1}{2}$ in) in from the ends and 2.5 cm (1 in) in from the sides. These holes will need to be countersunk, so that the screws are exactly flush with the surface of the boards.

6 Before you start screwing the boards on to the fixing battens on the legs, cut (plane) the tongue off the top board of each wall and the groove off the bottom one.

7 Apply glue to the battens and screw the boards into place. Do one wall first using two legs, and then make up a separate wall using the other two legs.

8 Join your two walls together with the boards for the third and fourth walls. Here, the battery powered screwdriver comes into its own, eliminating the blisters you always get when driving lots of screws in by hand.

9 Before the glue goes hard, check the box for squareness by measuring the diagonals. Adjust the box until the diagonals are equal.

10 Fit the two floor fixing battens to the bottom of opposite walls. These are fitted in the same way as the wall fixing battens.

Floor

1 The floor is made up of five lengths of standard floor-boarding. Plane off the groove of one length and the tongue off another. These will be the two outer planks.

2 Put the five boards together and 'offer' them up to the box legs. Mark how much you have to notch out of the ends of the outer planks to make them fit.

3 Turn the box upside down (be careful not to damage the tops of the legs) and cut the notch out of one plank and fit it. Fit the other middle planks and then check the size of the notch on the other outer plank. You may find that this plank is too wide and sticks out from under the box. If it is, plane it down to size before fitting.

4 Mark up two lines across the floorboards that line up with the centre of the fixing battens.

5 Remove all the planks and drill countersunk pilot holes for the screws.

6 Apply glue to the fixing battens and screw the floor into place.

7 The box is finished by fitting a capping strip round the top of the walls, and by fitting four blocks inside on which the trellis legs can rest themselves.

8 When all is fitted and the glue has set, drill some holes in the floor to facilitate drainage.

Trellis

1 This is made from 2.5 × 1.9 cm (1 × ¾ in) batten. Cut four identical lengths for the uprights. Then cut the various lengths of horizontal pieces.

2 Place the ends of the uprights on the resting blocks inside the box and hold their tops together. You will probably need an assistant for this. Tape the ends together to hold them in place.

3 Start fitting the horizontals. The lengths of the horizontals given in the cutting list (figure 13.2) are approximate, so you will probably find it easiest to fit and cut them as you go. Drill pilot holes to prevent

splitting the battens. Fit the top and bottom ones first because once you've done them the structure is more stable. The top, where all the uprights meet can be capped off with a pyramid or sphere shape to match the box leg tops.

Finishing

To hide the screw head on the box walls you can run beading around the inside of all four faces. You can use plain beading, or ornamental moulding and add stencilled patterns or carved ornamentation to the sides.

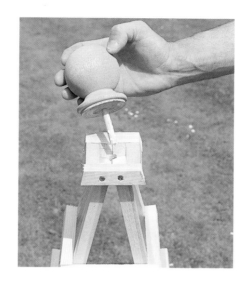

The pyramid trellis should be built *in situ* with its four feet resting on the supports inside the tub, and the other ends held together at the top giving a symmetrical shape.

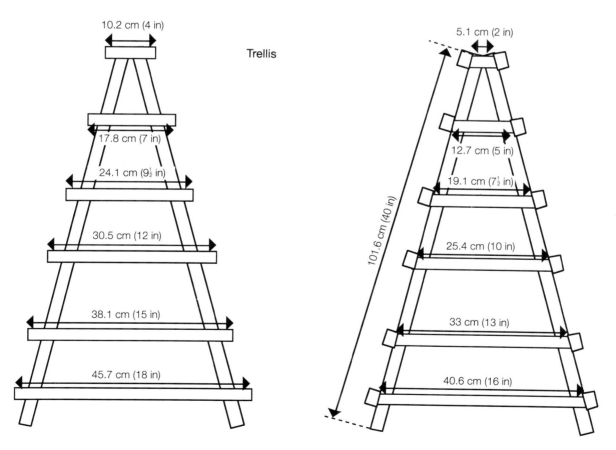

Trellis

10.2 cm (4 in)

17.8 cm (7 in)

24.1 cm (9½ in)

30.5 cm (12 in)

38.1 cm (15 in)

45.7 cm (18 in)

5.1 cm (2 in)

12.7 cm (5 in)

19.1 cm (7½ in)

25.4 cm (10 in)

33 cm (13 in)

40.6 cm (16 in)

101.6 cm (40 in)

FIGURE 13.2
Storage bench: cutting patterns 2

Poet's Seat

The lines of this lyrical composition – a poet's seat – are crafted to fit on the ends of the pergola, the final project in the book, though, of course, the poet's seat can equally well stand alone. Its high back, and trellised sides, provide a secluded hide-away for solitary contemplation of the wonders of nature, or a quiet read.

Construction

The seat is built in four stages, the frame, the roof, the seat, and the trellising. See figures 14.1 and 14.2 for cutting patterns. Brackets are used to fix this project together.

Tools and materials

- Pencil
- Flexible rule
- Set square
- Saw
- Drill
- Countersink bit
- Screwdriver
- 6 doz 3.8 cm (1½ in) No. 8 screws
- 300 ml pack waterproof glue
- 3 doz tacks
- Water-based wood stain preservative
- 4 flat connector brackets (No. 71001 Abru Joyners)
- 18 large angle brackets (No. 71007 Abru Joyners)

Timber cutting list

Part	Quantity	Dimensions (L × W × Th)
Frame	2 (Sawn timber)	213.4 × 7.6 × 5.1 cm 84 × 3 × 2 in
Frame	2 (Sawn timber)	180 × 7.6 × 5.1 cm 72 × 3 × 2 in
Frame	4 (Sawn timber)	61 × 7.6 × 5.1 cm 24 × 3 × 2 in
Frame	4 (Sawn timber)	50.8 × 7.6 × 5.1 cm 20 × 3 × 2 in
Roof	2 (Sawn timber)	74.9 × 5.1 × 2.5 cm 29½ × 2 × 1 in
Roof	1 (Sawn timber)	86.4 × 5.1 × 2.5 cm 34 × 2 × 1 in
Roof	2 (Sawn timber)	5.1 × 5.1 × 2.5 cm 2 × 2 × 1 in
Roof	2 (Sawn timber)	80 × 7.6 × 2.5 cm 31½ × 3 × 1 in
Roof	7 (Tongue and groove 'V' board)	86.4 × 10.2 × 2.5 cm 34 × 4 × 1 in
Roof	Cedar shingles	Enough to cover 0.28sq m (1 sq yd)
Seat	6 (Planed timber)	61 × 10.2 × 2.5 cm 24 × 4 × 1 in
Seat	1 (Planed timber)	74.9 × 10.2 × 2.5 cm 29½ × 4 × 1 in
Seat	1 (Battening)	61 × 10.2 × 2.5 cm 24 × 4 × 1 in
Seat back	6 (Planed timber)	101.6 × 10.2 × 2.5 cm 40 × 4 × 1 in
Seat back	2 (Planed timber)	61 × 10.2 × 2.5 cm 24 × 4 × 1 in
Seat back	1 (Planed timber)	61 × 5.1 × 2.5 cm 24 × 2 × 1 in
Trellis sides	26 (Battening)	50.8 × 2.5 × 2.5 cm 20 × 1 × 1 in
Trellis sides	2 (Battening)	34.3 × 2.5 × 2.5 cm 13½ × 1 × 1 in
Trellis sides	2 (Battening)	142.3 × 2.5 × 2.5 cm 56 × 1 × 1 in
Trellis sides	2 (Battening)	147.3 × 2.5 × 2.5 cm 58 × 1 × 1 in
Trellis sides	2 (Battening)	152.4 × 2.5 × 2.5 cm 60 × 1 × 1 in
Trellis sides	2 (Battening)	157.5 × 2.5 × 2.5 cm 62 × 1 × 1 in)
Trellis sides	2 (Battening)	162.6 × 2.5 × 2.5 cm 64 × 1 × 1 in

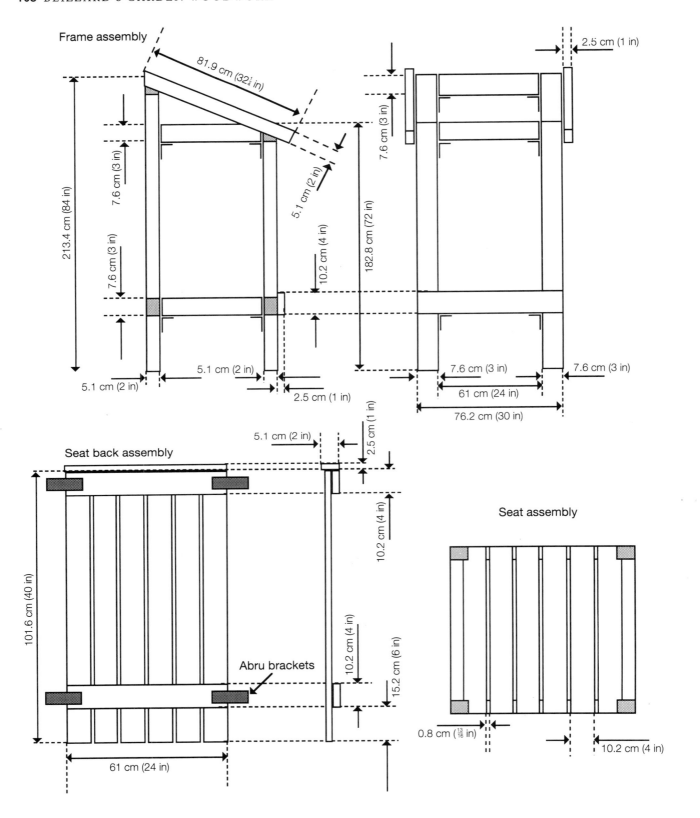

FIGURE 14.1 Poet's seat: cutting patterns 1

Frame

1 The frame is very similar to the frame of the pergola at the end of the book. It is made up of a rear section and a front section joined together by cross struts. It is constructed entirely in 7.6 × 5.1 cm (3 × 2 in) rough sawn timber. All the screws are cross head 3.8 cm (1½ in) No. 8s unless otherwise stated. The rear section is made first from two 213.4 cm (84 in) lengths and two 61 cm (24 in) lengths. Place the two 213.4 cm (84 in) pieces face down, side by side, 61 cm (24 in) apart, on a flat surface such as a garage floor. Place the first (top) 61 cm (24 in) piece across between them, flush to one end, and connect the three together using large 'L' shaped brackets on the inside angles.

2 The second (lower) 61 cm (24 in) piece is fitted 38.1 cm (15 in) in from the other end in the same way. These brackets should be on the 38.1 cm (15 in) side of the cross-piece.

3 The front section is constructed in exactly the same way but using 182.8 cm (72 in) lengths instead of the 213.4 cm (84 in) pieces.

4 The two sections are then joined together using four 50.8 cm (20 in) lengths. Lay the front section flat, and place the 50.8 cm (20 in) lengths on end, so that their 7.6 cm (3 in) sides line up flush with the join lines between the 182.8 cm (72 in) and 61 cm (24 in) members. Fix them with large 'L' brackets on to the 182.8 cm (72 in) lengths.

5 Stand the front frame against a wall with its four 50.8 cm (20 in) pieces protruding out horizontally. Offer up the back section so that it rests against these outer ends. The lower struts should line up and fix in the same spot as on the front section. The top of the upper strut should be 30.5 cm (12 in) down from the top, and its inner side flush with the inner side of the vertical. Again large 'L' brackets are used, positioned on the underside of the struts. When the frame is completed it looks rather like the frame for a tennis umpire's high chair.

Fixing the roof

1 Fit two 74.9 cm (29½ in) lengths of 5.1 × 2.5 cm (2 × 1 in) timber diagonally across between the top ends of the frame, one each side, from front to back. The top edges of these inner rails should be flush with the front corners of the verticals, and they should not stick out beyond the back of the rear frame. They are fixed to the outside faces of the frame with a screw through the ends of each piece into the frame.

2 Fix a 86.4 cm (34 in) piece of 5.1 × 2.5 cm (2 × 1 in) timber to the front ends of the two side pieces just fitted. Make sure that this front rail overlaps at each end by 2.5 cm (1 in). Make up two pieces of scrapwood 2.5 cm (1 in) thick (5.1 × 5.1 cm (2 × 2 in) will do nicely) to use as spacers. Each spacer is screwed on to the back end of one of the inner rails.

3 Fit two pieces of 7.6 × 2.5 cm (3 × 1 in) each 80 cm (31½ in) long, from the spacers down to the outer ends of the front rail. Ensure that these outer rail bottom edges are flush with the bottom of the inner rails.

4 Mark up and cut the upper (rear) end of these pieces to an angle which will be vertical when they are in place. These can now be fixed with screws through them into the spacers at one end and the ends of the front rail at the other.

5 The roof is now ready to cover. This is done firstly with 11.5 cm × 2.5 cm (4½ × 1 in) tongue and groove boarding. Cut seven 86.4 cm (34 in) lengths and fit starting at the front with the grooves on the top (rear) side. They should fit neatly between the outer rails. Screw them right down through the boards into the inner rails.

6 Then tile over the boarding using the roof shingles. These should be nailed down using 2.5 cm (1 in) zinced felt nails, starting at the front with a 9.6 cm (3¾ in) overhang. Leave

a gap of about 0.6 cm ($\frac{1}{4}$ in) between the tiles to allow for expansion. Each subsequent row should overlap the one below by 9.6 cm ($3\frac{3}{4}$ in). This completes the frame and roof.

Seat

1 Cut six pieces of 10.2 × 2.5 cm (4 × 1 in) planed timber to 61 cm (24 in). These should be fixed, running front to back, to the lower cross-members of the front and back frames. Note that the ends should be exactly flush with the outer faces of the cross-members, and they should be evenly spaced so that they are about 0.7 cm ($\frac{5}{16}$ in) apart.

2 Fit a 61 cm (24 in) piece of 2.5 × 2.5 cm (1 × 1 in) batten across, and 2.5 cm (1 in) in from the rear ends of the seat boards. It should fit neatly between the uprights of the rear frame.

3 To finish the base of the seat, fit a 76.2 cm (30 in) piece of 10.2 × 2.5 cm (4 × 1 in) board across the front of the front frame, covering the ends of the seat boards. The top edge of this should be flush with the tops of the seat boards. Sand the outer edge of this smooth and round for the 'poet's' comfort.

4 The back of the seat is supported by two 61 cm (24 in) pieces of 10.2 × 2.5 cm (4 × 1 in) fitted between the uprights of the rear frame. These seatback supports are fixed in position using four flat bracket connectors. The bottom edge of the lower one should be 15.2 cm (6 in) above the seat boards. The top edge of the top one should be flush with the top of the 101.6 cm (40 in) seat back planks fitted next.

5 Cut six 101.6 cm (40 in) lengths of 10.2 × 2.5 cm (4 × 1 in) and fit

them to the inside of the back supports. They should have the same spacing as the seat boards. They are fixed by screwing through the upper and lower back supports into the boards. Note that the lower ends of the boards should rest on the 2.5 × 2.5 cm (1 × 1 in) batten, and the top should be flush with the top of the top seat back support.

6 Cap the top ends of the boards using a 61 cm (24 in) length of 5.1 × 2.5 cm (2 × 1 in). This is fixed in position by screwing through into the top seat back support. That completes the main structure.

Trellis

1 The trellis is fitted directly on to the side frame of the seat. You start by fitting the five verticals – shortest at the front and progressively longer towards the rear. The bottom end of each vertical should be screwed to the outside of the bottom cross-member, overlapping by 2.5 cm (1 in) and the top end screwed to the inside of the inner rail of the roof. Fix the first batten 3.8 cm ($1\frac{1}{2}$ in) from the other side.

2 The exposed bottom ends of the verticals should be capped with 50.8 cm (20 in) batten to tidy them up neatly.

3 Fix twelve 50.8 cm (20 in) horizontal pieces to the inside of the verticals. Start with one 7.6 cm (3 in) down from the upper cross-member and space them by 7.6 cm (3 in) each.

4 Finally fix a 34.3 cm ($13\frac{1}{2}$ in) batten to the verticals above the upper cross-member.

5 The same procedure is used for the other side of the seat.

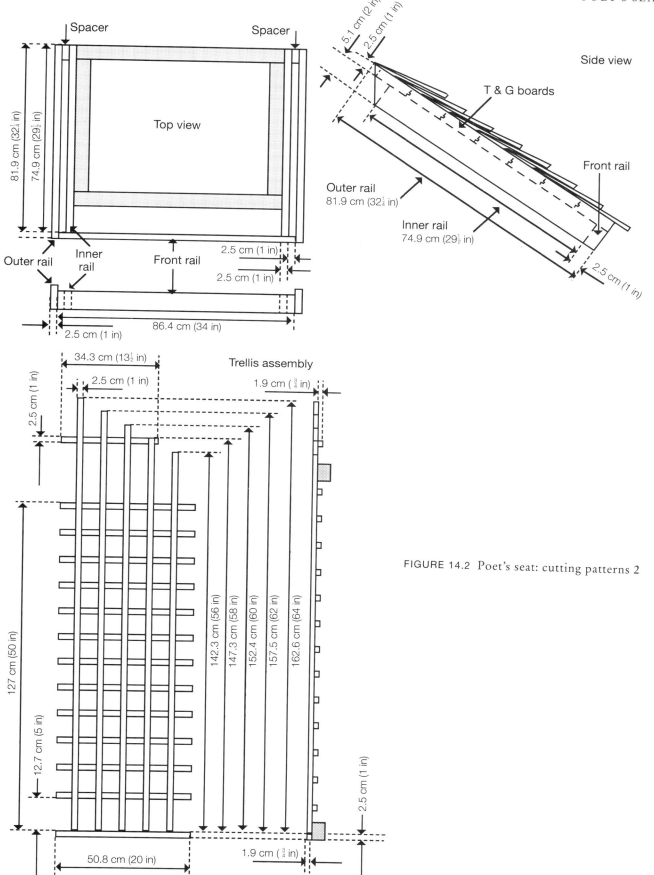

Spacer
Spacer

81.9 cm (32¼ in)
74.9 cm (29½ in)

Top view

2.5 cm (1 in)

Outer rail
Inner rail
Front rail

2.5 cm (1 in)

2.5 cm (1 in)
86.4 cm (34 in)

5.1 cm (2 in)
2.5 cm (1 in)

Side view

T & G boards

Front rail

Outer rail
81.9 cm (32¼ in)

Inner rail
74.9 cm (29½ in)

2.5 cm (1 in)

34.3 cm (13½ in)

2.5 cm (1 in)

Trellis assembly

1.9 cm (¾ in)

2.5 cm (1 in)

142.3 cm (56 in)
147.3 cm (58 in)
152.4 cm (60 in)
157.5 cm (62 in)
162.6 cm (64 in)

127 cm (50 in)

12.7 cm (5 in)

2.5 cm (1 in)

50.8 cm (20 in)

1.9 cm (¾ in)

FIGURE 14.2 Poet's seat: cutting patterns 2

Table and Bench

*The sturdy but simple table and
bench are easy to build, using only
screws and glue. There is no
woodworking beyond sawing planks
to length and drilling holes.*

Tools and materials

- Pencil
- Flexible rule
- Set square
- Saw
- Drill
- Countersink bit
- Screwdriver
- Plane
- 8 doz 3.8 cm (1½ in) No. 8 screws
- 300 ml pack waterproof glue
- Wood filler
- Moulding and brass tacks (optional)
- Water-based wood stain preservative

Timber cutting list

Part	Quantity	Dimensions (L × W × Th)
Table top	7 (Planking)	132.1 × 10.2 × 2.5 cm 52 × 4 × 1 in
Table frame sides	2 (Planking)	127 × 10.2 × 2.5 cm 50 × 4 × 1 in
Table frame cross-pieces	4 (Planking)	61 × 10.2 × 2.5 cm 24 × 4 × 1 in
Table legs	4 (Timber)	73.7 × 7.6 × 7.6 cm 29 × 3 × 3 in
Bench top	4 (Planking)	132.1 × 10.2 × 2.5 cm 52 × 4 × 1 in
Bench frame sides	2 (Planking)	127 × 10.2 × 2.5 cm 50 × 4 × 1 in
Bench frame cross-pieces	4 (Planking)	33.7 × 10.2 × 2.5 cm 13¼ × 4 × 1 in
Bench legs	4 (Timber)	45.7 × 7.6 × 5.1 cm 18 × 3 × 2 in

Construction

The construction of the table (see figure 15.1) and the bench (figure 15.2) is easiest if you can find a large flat surface to build them on. Another table, covered with a sheet of ply or something similar to protect it, would be an ideal working height.

Table frame and legs

1 Lay the two 127 cm (50 in) lengths parallel on the flat surface, about 76.2 cm (30 in) apart. They should be standing with the 2.5 cm (1 in) surface on the flat surface and the 10.2 cm (4 in) side vertical. Place the two 61 cm (24 in) lengths across between them, one at either end. Move them together to form a rectangle, with the longer lengths just overlapping the ends of the shorter lengths. You now have the outer frame members in place.

2 Place the other two 61 cm (24 in) lengths parallel to the two ends at ⅓ and ⅔ distance along the frame so the four 61 cm (24 in) lengths are equally spaced. Place each of the four legs vertically in each corner of the table frame.

3 The legs and frame are as they will be in the final assembly. In pencil number the leg, the short side and long side of the frame at each corner so that you can put the pieces back together exactly as they are now. Next mark up the position for all the screws on the outside of the frame. There should be four screws in a square formation at each end of each outer frame member. These fix into the legs. Position these corner screws so that they will be 1.9 cm (¾ in) from the edges of the frame wood, and the same from the edges of the leg wood. This is to prevent the wood from splitting as you drive the screws in. A further two screws, in a vertical line, fix into each end of the middle cross-pieces through the middle of the longer sides.

Mark up the positions for all of these on the outside of the frame with a pencil.

4 Disassemble the structure and drill the holes for the screws through the frames using a 3mm (⅛ in) bit. Then drill a deep counter-sink (about 0.45 cm (³⁄₁₆ in) deep). These can be filled later with a woodfiller to cover the screwheads.

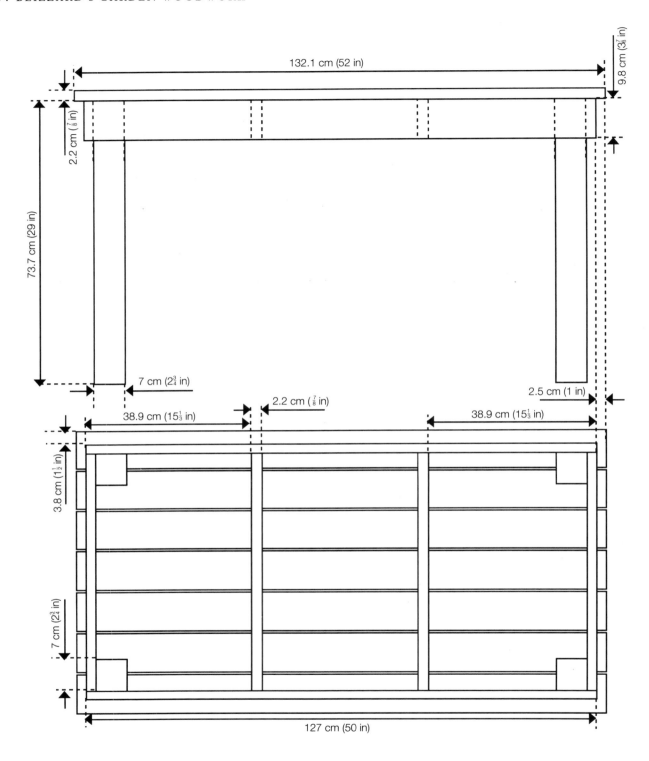

FIGURE 15.1 Table: cutting patterns

5 Reassemble the structure and drill the pilot holes for the screws through the holes in the frames using a 0.15 cm ($\frac{1}{16}$ in) bit.

6 Screw and glue the legs to the short frame members first. Check that the legs are at right-angles to the frame member.

7 Screw and glue the two end sections to the longer members, again checking the right angles.

8 Fit the two centre short cross members into position and screw and glue them into place. At this stage you should check that the diagonal distance between opposite corners is the same. This checks for squareness in the whole structure. If it is out of square push gently on the corners until you get it square. Leave the whole structure to set for at least 12 hours and don't be tempted to move it or turn it over to 'have a quick look!'

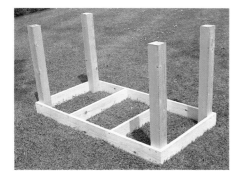

Table top

1 When the legs and frame structure is completely set turn it over on to its feet. To make the table top lay the seven planks out as they will be positioned in the finished table. To ensure the gap between the planks are the same, cut 12 spacers from 0.6 cm ($\frac{1}{4}$ in) thick wood such as 0.6 cm ($\frac{1}{4}$ in) ply, and place a spacer between each plank at each end. Make sure the planks are square and flush with each other, and that the overlaps at the ends and sides are equal.

2 Draw a thin pencil line across all the planks to mark the centre of the short cross-member underneath. This will ensure that your screws go into the middle of the cross-members, which are only 2.5 cm (1 in) wide so this is important. Number your planks so that you can put them back in order easily.

3 Mark the position for the screws. The planks that make up the table top are fitted using eight screws per plank. The screws fix into the four

short cross members of the frame, two screws into each cross member. All the screws except the outer ones of the two outer planks, are positioned 1.9 cm ($\frac{3}{4}$ in) from the edge and on the pencil lines. The outer ones need to be about 4.4 cm ($1\frac{3}{4}$ in) from the edge because the outer planks overlap the sides of the frame

4 When you have marked them to your satisfaction, disassemble the planks and drill the holes. Use the same countersink as you used for the holes for the frame.

5 Lay the planks out again in the correct position using the spacers. Check that the holes line up with the cross-members underneath. Drill pilot holes with a 0.15 cm ($\frac{1}{16}$ in) bit through the holes in the planks, down into the cross-members.

6 Remove the first plank and apply glue to the areas of the cross-members underneath. Screw it into position. Then work your way right across the table doing the same for each plank.

Finishing

1 Cover the countersunk screw heads with a wood filler. Use a two-pot product that can be planed, sanded and stained as the wood.

2 If you want to add trim around the top use plain 2.5 × 0.45 cm (1 × $\frac{3}{16}$ in) moulding chosen from the wood merchants. Butt the ends up against each other as you did for the frame members, and glue and tack it on using brass tacks (they don't rust). Rub down to rounded corners with sandpaper. The trim adds a bit of style, but isn't necessary so you can leave it out all together if you wish.

3 Treat the table with a non-toxic wood-stain preservative.

Bench

The bench is made in exactly the same way as the table. The legs for the bench are only 45.7 cm (18 in) long and are made of 7.6 × 5.1 cm (3 × 2 in) not 7.6 × 7.6 cm (3 × 3 in) and as the bench is narrower than the table, only four planks are used on its top.

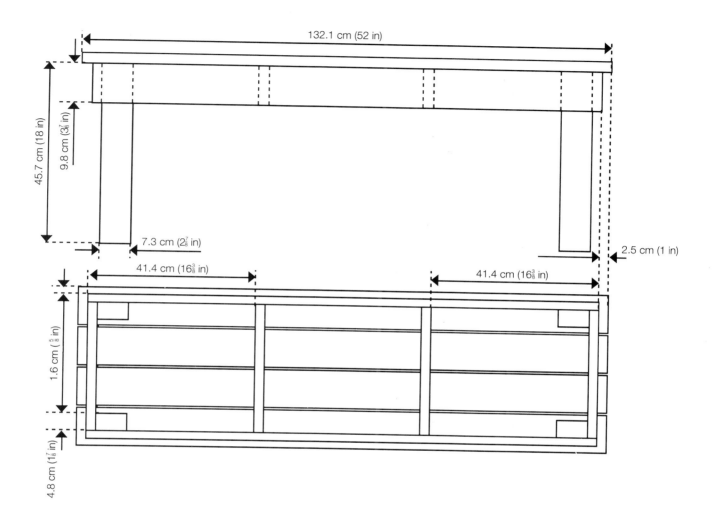

FIGURE 15.2 Bench: cutting patterns

Pergola

Nothing is more relaxing than sitting quietly in your garden on a warm summer's evening inhaling the fragrance of flowers and the heady scent of honeysuckle climbing over a wooden pergola. This pergola requires no woodworking skills beyond using a saw and a screwdriver, and is designed as two units which fit together in a number of ways to form different shapes.

Tools and materials

- Pencil

- Flexible rule

- Tape measure

- Set square

- Hand saw

- Electric drill

- Hack-saw

- Cross-head (Phillips) screwdriver, preferably battery powered (there are a lot of screws to put in!)

- Cross-head screw bit

- Drill bit, 1.5 mm ($\frac{1}{16}$ in), for pilot holes for screws

- Drill bit, 6 mm ($\frac{1}{4}$ in), for pilot holes for the coach screws

- Spirit level

- Adjustable spanner (for fitting coach screws)

- Spade (to dig holes for the feet)

- Step ladder

Module A

- 20 small 'L' shaped brackets (Abru Joyners No. 71009, brown)

- 8 large 'L' shaped brackets (Abru Joyners No. 71007, brown)

- 8 straight strapping brackets (Abru Joyners No. 71001, brown)

- 4 foot post anchor brackets (Abru Joyners No. 71018, brown)

- 400 3.8 cm ($1\frac{1}{2}$ in) No. 8 zinc-plated cross-headed screws. (Bear in mind that near the edge of timber, within 2.5 cm (1 in) it is still better to drill pilot holes to prevent any splitting of the wood.

- 8 7.6 × 1 cm (3 × $\frac{3}{8}$ in) coach screws

- Bag of ready-mix cement

- 3 litres of preservative

Module B

- 14 small 'L' shaped brackets (Abru Joyners No. 71009, brown)

- 4 large 'L' shaped brackets (Abru Joyners No. 71007, brown)

- 8 straight strapping brackets (Abru Joyners No. 71001, brown), four of them for joining module A to module B

- 2 foot post anchor brackets (Abru Joyners No. 71018, brown)

- 300 3.8 cm ($\frac{1}{2}$ in) No. 8 zinc-plated cross-headed screws

- 4 7.6 × 1 cm (3 × $\frac{3}{8}$ in) coach screws

- Bag of ready-mix cement

- 2 litres of preservative

Construction

The small basic unit, Module A, can be used by itself in the garden. By adding one or more of the extension Module B, you can achieve the shape and size of pergola that best suits your garden.

Module A has two pairs of legs joined across the top by a wooden ladder section. Module B is L shaped with the same wooden ladder top but only one set of legs. The overhangs on the ladder top are designed so that Module B will fit exactly on any corner of Module A to form a L shape or will fit lengthways to extend in a straight line. You can plug up to six module Bs into one A, two on each side and one on each end. You can then go on extending in any direction.

Timber cutting list: Module A

Part	Quantity	Dimensions (L × W × Th)
Top of legs	2 (Timber)	122 × 7.6 × 5.1 cm 48 × 3 × 2 in
Top ladder section	4 (Timber)	122 × 7.6 × 5.1 cm 48 × 3 × 2 in
Legs	4 (Timber)	213.4 × 7.6 × 5.1 cm 84 × 3 × 2 in
Top ladder section rails	2 (Timber)	244 × 7.6 × 5.1 cm 96 × 3 × 2 in
Brace at bottom of leg section	2 (Timber)	61 × 7.6 × 5.1 cm 24 × 3 × 2 in
Diagonal braces (ends cut at 45 degrees)	4 (Timber)	61 × 7.6 × 5.1 cm 24 × 3 × 2 in
Trellis verticals	6 (Roofing batten)	190.5 × 2.5 × 1.9 cm 75 × 1 × $\frac{3}{4}$ in
Lengths for horizontals	9 (Roofing batten)	76.2 × 2.5 × 1.9 cm 30 × 1 × $\frac{3}{4}$ in

Timber cutting list: Module B

Part	Quantity	Dimensions (L × W × Th)
Top of legs	1 (Timber)	122 × 7.6 × 5.1 cm 48 × 3 × 2 in
Top ladder section	4 (Timber)	122 × 7.6 × 5.1 cm 48 × 3 × 2 in
Legs	2 (Timber)	213.4 × 7.6 × 5.1 cm 84 × 3 × 2 in
Top ladder section rails	2 (Timber)	244 × 7.6 × 5.1 cm 96 × 3 × 2 in
Brace at bottom of leg section	1 (Timber)	61 × 7.6 × 5.1 cm 24 × 3 × 2 in
Diagonal braces (ends cut at 45 degrees)	2 (Timber)	61 × 7.5 × 5.1 cm 24 × 2 × 2 in
Trellis verticals	3 (Roofing batten)	190.5 × 2.5 × 1.9 cm 75 × 1 × $\frac{3}{4}$ in
Lengths for horizontals	9 (Roofing batten)	76.2 × 2.5 × 1.9 cm 30 × 1 × $\frac{3}{4}$ in

Cutting

1 The first thing to do is to cut your timber to length. Use a set square or an old triangular geometry protractor to mark right around the wood in pencil – then saw to the pencil marks. This will give you good square ends, which in turn will give you closer, stronger joints.

2 The diagonal braces with their 45 degree ends, are probably the trickiest to do well. Mark the ends with a 45 degree line, here again the protractor is ideal. Then mark in pencil down both sides of the wood to guide you as you cut. It's a good idea to practise this first on an old piece of timber.

Constructing the parts for module A

Legs

1 With the timber ready and cut to length you'll need a good flat surface to work on. Bearing in mind the lengths involved, a garage floor, driveway or lawn can be used.

2 Lay out two 2.1 m (7 ft) legs, a 1.2 m (4 ft) cross-piece and a bottom 0.6 m (2 ft) brace as shown in figure 16.1. The 7.6 × 5.1 cm (3 × 2 in) legs are laid with the 7.6 cm (3 in) surface on the ground. The legs should be parallel and 61 cm (24 in) apart. When you place the 1.2 m (4 ft) length symmetrically across the top you'll find you have a 22.9 cm (9 in) overhang each side. Check this, as it becomes important when you start plugging modules together. All the joins are made using Abru Joyner brackets, which are absolutely ideal for this type of construction. The 0.6 m (2 ft) brace fits exactly between the legs, with its lower edge 15.2 cm (6 in) from the bottom. It's a good idea to mark the joins with a pencil, in case you accidentally disturb the layout while fitting the brackets.

3 Offer the appropriate sized bracket up to each join and mark the screw holes with a pencil. Drill small pilot holes for the screws with the drill bit in your battery

screwdriver or electric drill. It doesn't need to go in very far, as this is just to get the screw started.

4 Fix in all the screws. This is where the value of cross-head screws becomes clear – the screwdriver bit stays in the screw-head, and the battery screwdriver can drive them in as fast as you can line them up.

5 Once you have put it together and are satisfied it's right, simply lay the pieces for the other legs on top and fix in the same way. This saves measuring up again.

Top ladder rack

1 Lay the two 7.6 × 5.1 cm (3 × 2 in) 2.4 m (8 ft) rails out on your flat surface, but this time with their 5.1 cm (2 in) surface on the ground. Again they are parallel and 61 cm (24 in) apart. Measure in 25.4 cm (10 in) from each end and mark with a pencil line. Place a 1.2 m (4 ft) length at each end, again with the 5.1 cm (2 in) side downwards, with the outside edge on the marks. Then measure 61 cm (24 in) to where the next cross-piece goes. Lay it on in the same way. Once you've got all four on, check that the gap between the two inner ones is 50.8 cm (20 in). As a check of the order, looking from the top you should have the first 25.4 cm (10 in) of rail, then 5.1 cm

(2 in) thickness of the first cross-piece, then 61 cm (24 in) of rail, then 5.1 cm (2 in) of second cross-piece, then 50.8 cm (20 in) of rail, then 5.1 cm (2 in) of third cross-piece, then 61 cm (24 in) of rail, then 5.1 cm (2 in) of the last cross-piece and finally the last 25.4 cm (10 in) of rail. This adds up to 2.4 m (8 ft). Mark it up in case you disturb it.

2 Each cross-piece is fixed with two of the smaller 'L' shaped brackets. You get a more rigid structure by putting them on opposite sides of the cross-piece, one on each rail.

3 If you are building more than one module, build all the top sections on top of each other to save measuring and marking them up.

The top ladder rack for module B is exactly the same as for module A.

Constructing the parts for module B

For module B you need only one set of legs, (see figure 16.2) constructed in the same way as module A.

Timber preservation

Use a water-based timber preservative to treat the wood. This will not harm plants, animals or soil once it is dry.

Module A
7.6 × 5.1 cm (3 × 2 in) sawn timber.
(No brackets shown)

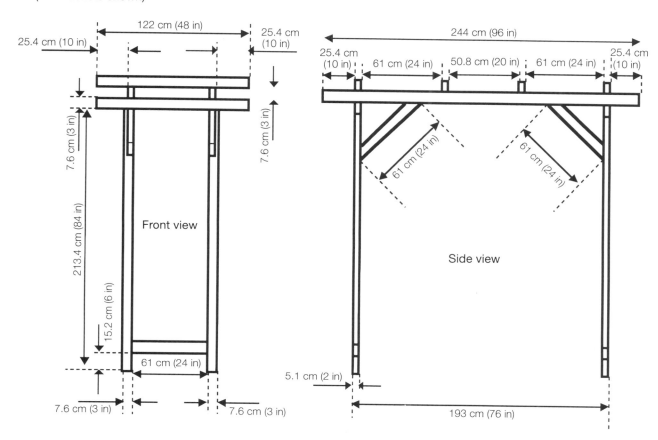

FIGURE 16.1 Pergola: cutting patterns 1

Assembling module A

1 The module is easiest to build inverted, so place the top section on the ground with the cross-pieces down. The top cross-pieces of the legs are then placed on the rails directly above the end cross-pieces of the top section. Make sure they really are lined up directly above them.

2 Get someone to hold the legs vertical in the air while you fix them on using four of the larger 'L' shaped brackets on each leg section.

3 Check over the structure and make sure you have at least eight to ten screws in each bracket. Abru

brackets have dozens of holes, but you don't need to fill them all.

4 When you have finished, turn the structure over on to its legs. A flat surface to put it on is helpful here. Make sure the legs are at 90 degrees to the top, and that it all looks square. Fit the diagonals as snuggly as you can with the 45 degree surfaces flat on the top rail and the inside surface of the leg.

5 Fix with straight strap brackets. It saves time to fix a bracket at each end of the diagonal before you start, which only leaves you the screws to go into the leg and rail when you have everything lined up.

Assembling module B

Module B is assembled in exactly the same way as module A but with only one set of legs.

Module B
7.6 × 5.1 cm (3 × 2 in) sawn timber.
(No brackets shown)

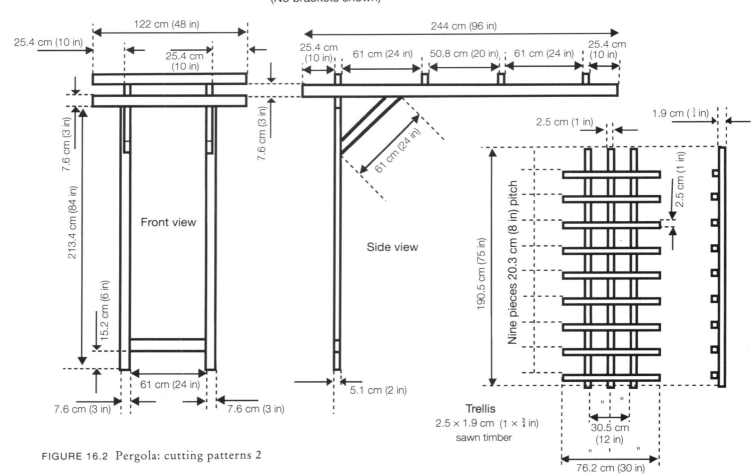

FIGURE 16.2 Pergola: cutting patterns 2

Feet brackets

1 When the preservative has dried, you can fit the 1.2 m (4 ft) post anchor brackets to the feet. These brackets bolt on to the legs and have a long steel rod protruding from the bottom. Because the brackets are designated for 7.6 cm (3 in) square timber this timber is 7.6 × 5.1 cm (3 × 2 in) you have to adapt them slightly. You will see that the part without the steel rod has a tongue which slides into the other part. You need to shorten that tongue by 2.5 cm (1 in) so that the bracket will clamp up tight on the 7.6 × 5.1 cm (3 × 2 in). Do this with a hack-saw – the bracket is mild steel so cuts very easily.

2 Two coach screws are used to fix each bracket, using a top hole on one side and a bottom hole on the other, so that the screws don't meet in the middle! It's vital to drill pilot holes for these otherwise the wood will split.

Setting module A in the ground

1 With someone to assist you stand the structure up in the position you want it, and mark where the feet touch the ground.

2 Lift it to one side and dig a 22.9 cm (9 in) square hole about 30.5 cm (12 in) deep. Put a small slab or stones at the bottom of each hole for the steel rod on the feet to rest on.

3 By adding or removing stones from underneath you can get the whole structure level. Check it with a spirit level if possible. If not walk around the structure and do it by eye.

4 Mix up your ready-mix cement and fill the holes to the top of the steel rods. This leaves the wooden

foot clear of the ground and less prone to rot. If you are doing more than one module, get the A module fixed up securely and level before adding the next.

5 One important job before the cement goes off is to make sure everything looks square and level from all angles. Unscrew the bottom of the diagonal braces from the legs, and someone to assist you, view from various angles, adjusting until everyone agrees it looked right! Then refix the diagonals.

Trellises

1 The trellises are made from the roofing batten. You'll find it a lot easier to paint these with preservative before you make them, rather than afterwards. Lay the lengths out together on the ground and paint one side. Turn them and then paint the next side.

2 Don't be tempted to nail these – they will split. Drill pilot holes and screw them together. Build the trellis by drilling the ends of the 76.2 cm (30 in) horizontals, and fitting them at regular intervals all the way down the legs.

3 Fix the verticals to the top and bottom horizontal pieces.

4 Drill and put screws into as many of the other junctions as are necessary to make the trellis rigid. Note that the verticals look better if they are fitted to the inside of the horizontals.

Fitting modules A and B together

1 You can fit module B either on the side or the end of module A. To use B to extend the length of your

pergola you simply butt the ends of the top rails of the two modules together and put two straight strapping brackets across the join. To make the join extra strong you can overlap the ends and then fit strapping brackets.

2 Cement the feet in the ground as described and adjust the level before final fixing.

3 You can add further B modules on either end in the same way, until you have exactly the length you want.

4 If you want to add module B on to the side of A you fit the end of one rail of B into the gap between A's end top cross-piece and the leg top piece. The B's other rail end will then fit neatly under the next cross-piece along.

5 Again use straight strapping brackets to fix them together, and cement the feet in the ground.

6 By adding to ends and sides you can produce zig-zags, large 'L' shapes, rectangles or squares. It's worth noting that if you fit two B's on the same side of an A (one at each end), the ends of the B's top cross-pieces butt up against each other in the middle. This gives the rather useful effect of a completely joined up roof, covering an area of 2.4 × 3.6 m (8 × 11 ft 2 in). This is a good size under which to position your table and chairs, as well as tubs, shrubs, pots or planters.

Index